TO CATCH A KILLER

TO CATCH A KILLER

MY HUNT FOR THE TRUTH BEHIND
THE DOORSTEP MURDER

PETER
BLEKSLEY

JOHN BLAKE

Published by John Blake Publishing,
2.25, The Plaza,
535 Kings Road,
Chelsea Harbour,
London SW10 0SZ

www.johnblakebooks.com

www.facebook.com/johnblakebooks ▪
twitter.com/jblakebooks ▪

This edition published in 2018

ISBN: 978 1 78 606 983 2

British Library Cataloguing-in-Publication Data:

A catalogue record for this book is available from the British Library.

Design by www.envydesign.co.uk

Printed and bound in Great Britain by Clays Ltd, Elcograf S.p.A.

1 3 5 7 9 10 8 6 4 2

© Text copyright Peter Bleksley 2018

Papers used by John Blake Publishing are natural, recyclable products made
from wood grown in sustainable forests. The manufacturing processes conform
to the environmental regulations of the country of origin.

John Blake Publishing is an imprint of Bonnier Books UK
www.bonnierbooks.co.uk

To Sarah, my wife, my life, my everything.

ACKNOWLEDGEMENTS

An enormous number of people have helped me with my research into this tragic murder. Many of these wonderful human beings have sworn me to secrecy over their identities in order to protect their livelihoods, their reputations, their relationships and more.

Some of the country's leading experts have given their time freely. Other kind-spirited people have helped me to generate publicity around this crime, which in turn has persuaded some brave people to come forward and talk to me.

Generous souls have helped with my research, put the kettle on or opened a bottle of Scotland's finest malt whisky, over which we have dissected the evidence, the theories, the gossip and the rumours, and then worked up a strategy.

Friends and family have had to suffer my endless fascination with this dreadful killing. They have done so without complaint and often with significant input.

Whatever your role in all of this has been, please rest assured that I could not have written this book without you. I remain forever indebted to you all.

CONTENTS

PROLOGUE

Towards the end of November 2005, the phone rang. It was a BBC radio journalist based in Scotland, who I'd met on my travels earlier in the year. I'd been in Glasgow researching a crime that remains unsolved to this day, the battering to death of Alexander Blue in 2002. This journalist and I had got on well. He knew my passion for trying to move unsolved cases forward and asked if I was aware of the murder of Alistair Wilson, which had taken place in Nairn in the Scottish Highlands in 2004. I knew the case quite well – I'd read almost every written word about the slaughter and there had been an enormous amount of publicity on the one-year anniversary, just a couple of days beforehand.

The way in which Alistair was gunned down on his front doorstep chimed loudly with me. While living in the witness protection programme I often feared being greeted by an assassin's bullet on my doorstep, and although my undercover police career was now some years behind me, some demons take longer than others to shrug off. My two young sons were very similar in age to Alistair's boys, another uncomfortable coincidence. I didn't realise then that this crime would enter my life and dominate so much of it.

The journalist asked if I would be willing to travel to Nairn to research and comment on the crime for BBC Radio 5 Live. The intention was that we'd start our research as soon as I landed in Scotland and that we'd comment live on air, twice a day, for three days in a row. I could not say yes quickly enough.

While money has never been my main motivation, I was delighted that the BBC agreed to pay me £250 a day. In four days, I was to earn the equivalent to what I'd pocketed for a year's work on other unsolved murders. My wife had recently begun a two-year career break from the police force so she could enjoy a couple of pre-school years with our boys. I'd been a full-time house husband since they were born, so losing Sarah's police salary for two years had been a massive financial hit. I had to start earning some cash and this work was going to be very welcome.

A few days later, I was on a plane heading to Inverness. The journalist met me at the airport. In the car to our hotel we discussed everything that we had gleaned from reports on the crime. He was keen to pick my former detective brain, asking me what I thought and if I had any firm theories. I was keeping an open mind although what I told him then remains true to this day: I strongly believe that the murder of Alistair Wilson is a crime that could, and should, be solved.

The hotel was somewhat luxurious, by far the best accommodation I was ever to stay in on any of my subsequent trips to Nairn and I very much doubt the BBC would foot the bill for that kind of hotel nowadays. We dumped our bags, grabbed a coffee and headed to the scene of the crime.

The reports that we filed from Nairn were enjoyable to do, albeit the subject material was very dark. We focused on different aspects of the crime every day – the scene, the suspect, the victim, the gun and more. The BBC seemed happy with my contribution.

The more I researched the case, the more I found it mystifying that the police had not arrested anyone for this crime. After all, they had his widow Veronica's eyewitness account, they'd recovered the murder weapon, and even though I'd heard that the murder scene had been contaminated by Uncle Tom Cobley and all traipsing through it, I was still very surprised that no one had had their collar felt.

I was a bit puzzled that a computer-generated image of the gunman had not been compiled and circulated, using Veronica's recollections of him. Perhaps her doorstep encounter was so brief, so fleeting, she could not provide enough detail. Maybe the events of that fateful evening were so traumatic that her recall was not what it otherwise would have been.

Call me old-fashioned, call me naive, but all I have ever sought to discover about this mystifying murder is the truth. If you find the truth, the evidence will take care of itself.

I thought the police might welcome my efforts – after all, I have a bit of a profile which might encourage people to speak. As an investigative writer I'm not so constrained as police officers might sometimes be, I'm free to go wherever my inclinations might take me. Besides, don't we all want the same thing? But I could not have been more wrong. The police refuse to answer my questions, even when those questions are as straightforward and uncontroversial as, 'Is there any current reward on offer for information relating to Alistair Wilson's murder?'

I thought the bank that Alistair worked for might cooperate with me. They would surely like to see someone brought to justice for shooting dead one of their employees. I called them and at their request, emailed a list of questions and, you've guessed it, they refused to answer any of them.

I thought Veronica might talk to me. Let's face it, the police have had fourteen long years in which to catch her husband's killer and they have manifestly failed, so I thought she might see the value in contributing to a book that would essentially be the longest 'Wanted' poster ever written. When I wrote to her, she didn't reply. I made a request for an interview through the police. I gave them a copy of my previous book, *On the Run*, to forward to Veronica. That book was about a number of unsolved murders and detailed how I'd dealt with bereaved families. I'd even managed to confront a cold-blooded killer in a car park. What more persuading could she need? Plenty, it would appear.

Any sane writer who fails to secure the cooperation of the three main protagonists in any given story would surely give up and move on to something else. Well, not me. These refusals merely served as red rags to a rather determined bull. I wondered what grubby little secrets the police or the bank might be harbouring that they didn't want me to uncover. I still hope to this day that Veronica will one day change her mind and talk to me, for I am so firmly committed to finding the truth that I will not cease until whosoever is responsible for this murder is put where they belong, firmly behind bars.

CHAPTER ONE

A STRANGER COMES CALLING

The Scottish Highland seaside town of Nairn came to prominence in Victorian times. Back in its heyday, royalty would come to stay. The actor Charlie Chaplin could be spotted around town, enjoying his holidays. Others were drawn there by the fact that Nairn enjoys a more temperate climate than many Highland locations and occupies an idyllic spot on the coast of the Moray Firth. There are many areas of stunning beauty within easy reach, including Loch Ness. The dolphins, birds and other wildlife are an attraction for many. Gloriously unspoilt, the beach stretches for miles. Inverness Airport is a mere ten-minute drive away. If driving is your thing, there are hundreds of miles of uncluttered road with breathtaking views to enjoy.

The overwhelming majority of Nairn residents that I have met have been faultlessly polite, generous and hospitable and only too happy to talk. Strangers will say good morning as they pass you in the street. Some people actually leave their front doors unlocked when they go out. I kid you not, for I've seen it with my own eyes. Communal spaces are well-tended and the verges and lawns look resplendent. The population of the town is about 10,000, which swells to around 11,000 if the outer-lying areas are factored in. As with any small town, some people are known to many, some are known to all and others keep themselves very much to themselves. I absolutely love the place and a framed print of the town adorns my office wall.

Of course Nairn has its issues. The high street is in need of investment in order to attract businesses to some of the shops that lie empty. Illegal drugs can be sourced fairly easily, if you're so minded, but I think the same can be said these days of just about every corner of the UK. There are small pockets of social deprivation, but this is a town unused to murder. The last killing that could be remembered by locals was the result of a fight following a wedding party, back in the mid-1990s. Overall, it's a wonderful place with the people to match. I would recommend it as a destination for a weekend away or a holiday in a heartbeat. If golf is your thing, you are in for a treat.

Not surprisingly perhaps, Alistair and Veronica Wilson chose it as the place to raise their young family. In 2002, they paid £162,100 for an imposing three-storey, double-fronted sandstone house that dominates Crescent Road. Rising high above the other properties in the road, the nine towering chimney pots of number 10 give an indication as to how many rooms lie within. In the past it had been a hotel, and Alistair and Veronica would later give the hospitality industry a try.

Crescent Road is separated from the beach by a row of small houses and the grassy links where locals walk their dogs. In summer, the local cricket club play matches on a part of the links that has been adapted. A three-minute walk from what was once Alistair's front door would find you with sand beneath your feet.

Crescent Road is only about 160 metres long from end to end. As you walk down it from the main road, which is the A96, on the left there is a short row of houses, a large bed-and-breakfast establishment, then there's Alistair's house. Two or three smaller houses complete the road on that side. On the opposite side, almost directly in front of Alistair's house, is what used to be known as The Havelock House Hotel. Nowadays, virtually everybody refers to it as 'The Havelock'. Essentially, it is a bar, with a few letting rooms above. There is a small restaurant area on the ground floor, although this is mainly used as the breakfast room for any staying guests. The Havelock has outside decking, benches and tables, and an adjoining car park, which can take about ten cars. The car park entrance is directly opposite Alistair's front door.

After The Havelock there is a small row of terraced houses and then what is now called The Braeval Hotel. At the time of Alistair's death in 2004, this was known as The Shambles Bar. Crescent Road is just about wide enough for two cars to pass one another; there are no pavements. The street lighting is adequate, no more than that – the road is certainly not bathed in artificial light. Crescent Road and the town of Nairn would soon be illuminated by the media spotlight in a way that it had never experienced before.

On Sunday, 28 November 2004, Alistair and Veronica took their children (two boys aged two and four) for a walk in the woods near to their home. They were also babysitting an eighteen-month-old child for some friends. The weather was pretty unremarkable, temperatures were slightly above average for that time of the year and all seemed well. The boys had a go on the swings and by the time early evening came, the family were at home, the boys being bathed and prepared for bed. Outside, the moon was 97 per cent visible, so to the untrained eye it would appear to be a full moon. The parents of the eighteen-month-old were apparently due any minute to collect their child. Veronica was hanging up the damp towels and Alistair was about to read the boys a bedtime story. During the week, Alistair worked some sixteen miles away in the city of Inverness, so when he got home there was often only time for a bath and the bedtime story, the recounting of which Al (as Veronica called him) had made his own. The family were together on the first floor of their home. Upstairs, in the self-contained flat occupying the top floor of the house, Veronica's stepdad, Ronald MacDonald, was relaxing.

Just after seven o'clock, the front doorbell rang. Veronica left Alistair in charge of the boys and made her way downstairs. When she opened the door, she saw a man who she initially described as 'white, clean-shaven, 5 foot, 4 inches to 5 foot, 8 inches tall, of stocky build, wearing a dark, waist-length, blouson-style jacket and a dark baseball cap'.

The man asked to speak to Alistair Wilson. Veronica returned upstairs to the first floor to tell her husband about this caller. Alistair apparently expressed some surprise that somebody would come to their front door at this time on a

Sunday evening, but undeterred and clearly unaware of what might lay in store, he went downstairs. He and this man then had a conversation on the doorstep. From her position upstairs Veronica could only describe the conversation as 'muffled'.

After a couple of minutes Alistair closed the front door and returned upstairs to Veronica. In his hand he was holding a blue envelope, the kind you might get when buying a greetings card. The envelope was open, with nothing inside, but it had the name 'Paul' on the outside. Veronica told the BBC in November 2017 that Alistair 'was just a bit bewildered as to what the gentleman had said, because the envelope wasn't addressed to him.' She continued, 'He was bewildered by the name, that it was not addressed to himself and there was nothing in the envelope. And I said, "No, he definitely asked for you by name."'

Veronica said neither she nor Alistair sensed any danger at this point – 'It wasn't threatening, it was just very unusual. But there was no fear, otherwise I wouldn't have let him go back downstairs. He didn't need to, he was in the house now.'

Veronica suggested she and Alistair should get the boys down for the night and then try to figure it all out. But Alistair's inquisitiveness appeared to get the better of him as she went on to say, 'He just said he'd go back downstairs and see if the gentleman was still there.'

Tragically, Alistair returned to the front door, which he opened. There was more conversation and once again, Veronica could not hear clearly. She then heard what she described as the sound of wooden pallets dropping to the ground. She went to investigate and found her husband lying prostrate on the ground, sprawled across the threshold of their home. Shot three times, he had been mortally wounded. Veronica spotted the gunman disappearing to her left, down Crescent Road in the direction of The Shambles Bar. She was unable to recall if he was running or walking.

Records show that at 7.11 p.m., Veronica dialled 999. In her understandable panic she ran the few short paces across the road to the doors of The Havelock. When she looked in, she didn't see anyone she recognised, so she returned to Alistair. The Wilsons' eldest son, who was only four at the time, had started to come downstairs. Veronica yelled to her stepfather, who by now had been alerted to the commotion, to take the boy out of sight of the unfolding horror. While instructions were being given to Veronica by the 999 call handler, she returned again to The Havelock and this time yelled for help. People came running; some wanted to help. Meanwhile, in The Shambles Bar, the owner of The Havelock, Andy Burnett, was having a drink. As word of the shooting quickly spread, Burnett thought he'd take a look at what was going on.

At 7.19 p.m. the ambulance arrived and the 999 call ended. Alistair was soon loaded on to a stretcher. As the ambulance crew tried to negotiate the six steep and unforgiving stone steps leading down from the path at the front of the Wilsons' home to the road, Alistair's prone body slipped from the stretcher. Veronica let out a piercing shriek.

A couple of journalists who lived nearby were soon at the scene, one of whom contacted his newsdesk. They were disbelieving. Nairn? Someone gunned down on their doorstep? Surely not.

Alistair was taken by ambulance to Raigmore Hospital in Inverness, where the staff did all they could to save his life. But it was not to be.

So began the most expensive, exhaustive and ultimately baffling murder inquiry the Northern Constabulary had ever embarked upon.

CHAPTER TWO

A NEW VENTURE

Alistair Wilson was born on 4 March 1974, in Ayrshire, Scotland. He was a second child for Alan and Joan, and a baby brother for their daughter Jillian. The family lived in Beith, a small town with a population of only 6,000 people, which was situated about twenty miles from Glasgow.

Alistair appears to have enjoyed a happy and fairly uneventful childhood. He attended Beith Primary School and then Garnock Academy. His English teacher there, John Hodgart, told *The Scotsman* newspaper in 2005 that Alistair was 'quiet, good-natured' and that he was also 'very well-mannered and respectful of authority'. Jamie Thorburn, an old school friend, described the teenage Alistair to the same newspaper: 'He was the type of guy who wouldn't go out until after he'd done his homework. He was also very focused. He knew even then he wanted to work for the bank.'

After leaving Garnock Academy, Alistair attended Stirling

University, graduating in 1996 with a degree in Accounting and Business Law. Not long after that, he began working for the Bank of Scotland. His first posting was to Fort William, another small town with a population of some 10,000 people. It was here that he met Veronica, a local lass who worked as a graphic designer. They fell in love and were married a couple of years later.

Not long afterwards Alistair was transferred to Edinburgh, where he worked in the private finance initiative and specialist lending department of the bank. In 1999, he was transferred to the bank's offices in Inverness, where his title became business banking manager. In the time leading up to his death he was responsible for bringing small to medium-sized businesses to the bank.

Perhaps not surprisingly, the media has been almost exclusively positive when describing Alistair. He has been repeatedly portrayed as a decent family man. Among the many photographs that have appeared in the press, there is one heartrending picture of Alistair cradling one of his newborn sons. Detective Chief Inspector Peter McPhee, a senior police officer on the inquiry, of whom you will hear more, described the victim as 'an upstanding member of the community'. Simon Cole-Hamilton, then chief executive of the Inverness Chamber of Commerce, told *Scotland on Sunday* that Alistair was 'a nice, approachable person…'

The word 'ambitious' would often crop up in describing Alistair. His sister Jillian told BBC *Crimewatch* in December 2004 that Alistair was 'an ambitious, hard-working man, a lot of people knew him and respected him. He just adored his wife and doted on his two wee sons'. The Provost of Nairn,

(A role somewhat equivalent to that of a borough mayor in Scotland), Mr Sandy Park, commented, 'I found him to be a very interesting, ambitious man.'

A clear sign of Alistair's ambition could be seen on 3 December 2002, when a full-page advert appeared in one of the local papers, the *Nairnshire Telegraph*. The banner headline declared, 'Make Lothian House Your Christmas Choice'. Lothian House was the name under which Alistair and Veronica's house, 10 Crescent Road, had previously operated as a restaurant and hotel. Now, they were reprising the name and launching their new business venture. The advert told how Alistair and Veronica, together with Veronica's stepbrother, Iain MacDonald, now the restaurant chef, were looking to put 10 Crescent Road 'on the dining and accommodation map'. The décor was described as 'clean, tasteful' and the advert told how the 'restaurant, lounge and bedrooms combine modern style with Scottish traditional values'. Clearly, the couple had put some considerable effort into preparing their venture for this big launch and advertising campaign. I suspect there must have been some investment in order to get everything up to scratch. The Scottish Tourist Board had awarded Lothian House the Small Hotel Three Crowns classification.

Alistair and Veronica told how they were hoping to appeal to dining guests and short-break holidaymakers, although Alistair stressed the whole venue was 'available for functions and parties who want to stay over'.

Iain MacDonald was described as 'the power behind the kitchen' and the piece went on to tell how he had spells working as a baker and butcher. Being December, the advert told how Christmas was the main theme of the menu, but aside from roast turkey, honey-glazed duck breast with cranberry and clementine marmalade and lemon salmon fillet were also available. Vegetarian options, a melange of vegetables and a wide range of starters and desserts were all on offer to the discerning guest. The article boasted, 'A comprehensive list of fine wines completes the offering'. All this must have required some considerable investment – fine wines do not come cheap!

A smiling Alistair was pictured alongside Veronica and Iain, who both beamed into the camera's lens. One of the letting rooms was shown alongside a photograph of the restaurant, which could cater for up to twenty-four guests. A four-course evening meal could be yours for £18.95, while a four-course lunch would set you back £12.50.

I have long harboured serious reservations about the wisdom of Alistair Wilson embarking on this business venture. For a start, I believe there was potential for a conflict of interest between Lothian House and his work for the Bank of Scotland. As stated earlier, part of his day job was to bring small and medium-sized businesses to the bank. I've spoken to a couple who operated a small hotel and restaurant almost identical to Lothian House, little more than a stone's throw away from Crescent Road. They had met Alistair a number of times as he was trying to persuade them to change banks, yet at the same time they were in direct competition as both they and Alistair tried to attract the same sort of customer base to their respective hospitality businesses. In the end this couple didn't take their custom to the Bank of Scotland, perhaps because they didn't want the owner of a business they were in direct competition with knowing all about their financial affairs. An unscrupulous bank employee (and there were a few of them, of whom you will learn later), also in competition with other local and similar businesses, could pore over a competitor's accounts, seeing what their turnover was, how much they charged clients, what they paid suppliers and probably more. The couple I met have stayed profitably in business ever since. Surely Alistair had to tell his employers about his new business interest?

Lothian House did not thrive under Alistair and Veronica's stewardship. Clearly, they had both hoped the business would succeed because in March 2003, Veronica had applied for, and been granted, a three-year licence to serve alcohol.

I have a number of friends who work in the hospitality trade. I've stayed in their fabulous hotels, eaten their outstanding food and enjoyed their beverages, be it remarkable coffee or an alcoholic drink or three. I have seen how tirelessly they graft, morning, noon and night, to make their businesses a success. Numerous sacrifices have to be made; the hours are notoriously antisocial, margins can be tight, suppliers are often challenging to deal with and you always have to put on a smile and an accommodating attitude towards customers who can sometimes be difficult. It is hard and unforgiving work, most definitely not a career path for the faint-hearted or a part-timer.

Throw a young family into the mix, Alistair working full-time in a demanding role at the bank, of which you will hear more later, and the fact there was a raft of competing businesses within the same geographical area, and I'm not hugely surprised that the Wilsons' business venture failed.

A close associate of Veronica told me that the business only ran for about nine months and that it 'fizzled out' rather than ending in some dramatic collapse. No company records were ever filed so it is not possible to ascertain what turnover there was during the brief reinvention of Lothian House. Whatever costs or debts were incurred, if indeed there were any such debts, they did not result in any legal action or bankruptcy that I can discover.

I wonder how disappointed, disillusioned or otherwise affected Alistair may have been by this unsuccessful venture. There has been a lot of media discussion about his private life, but nothing salacious, scandalous or offensive has ever been published. DCI McPhee, speaking on the first anniversary of the murder, stated categorically, 'The question of possible infidelities was something we had to look at, but there was nothing. We have not found a dark side to him. If there was, we would have expected to find it by now.'

Alistair did not make a will before he died, so Veronica had to submit a formal application to the Sheriff Court in Inverness in order to be appointed executor of his estate. This process took about a year, after which she then inherited Alistair's half share of the family home (the house was now valued at around £230,000), £6,243.91 from his personal bank account, £4,940.04 in bonuses due from the Bank of Scotland, £2,600 from savings schemes Alistair had joined, plus tax rebates, and some £2,000 of furniture and personal effects. Clearly Veronica had not inherited a fortune as a result of her husband's murder.

CHAPTER THREE

THE ERRORS UNFURL

It must have been hugely frustrating for the police that no living person apart from Veronica Wilson could testify to seeing the baseball cap-wearing gunman in Crescent Road. After all, there were bars with drinkers in them at both ends of Crescent Road and it would appear that the gunman had spent several minutes on the Wilsons' front doorstep. But despite exhaustive house-to-house inquiries and numerous media appeals, no one could help the police with that aspect of the inquiry.

However, some people had seen a man matching the gunman's description elsewhere in Nairn on that fateful night. A local resident, Tommy Hogg, told both the police and the media that he had seen a similarly dressed and suspiciously behaving individual on a bus from Inverness to Nairn just before the shooting happened. The man had got off the bus in Nairn and the timings all fitted. Mr Hogg gave a thorough statement to police.

This man was also seen by another local, a woman I have spoken to at length. She was waiting at the bus stop in town with her daughter, who was going to catch the bus back to university. The mum first spotted the man on the bus as it pulled up to the stop. She was so alarmed at the sight of this shifty and unpleasant-looking character that she was mightily relieved when he got off the bus and walked away – she had not wanted her daughter to board the bus, had this man stayed on it. After seeing news items and police appeals for information about Alistair's murder, she too came forward and gave a statement to the police.

The police re-interviewed the woman at her home a couple of weeks later. By this time, as part of their wider inquiries, they had checked all the transactions at local cashpoints and they questioned the woman about a £20 withdrawal made from a cashpoint in the High Street, while on her way to the bus stop. Apparently, she withdrew the money to give to her daughter without her partner's knowledge. Don't we all like to treat our kids? Now, her little secret was out. Fortunately, her partner saw the funny side.

In 2005, DCI McPhee told the media that the baseball-cap wearing man had been traced and almost certainly eliminated from the inquiry. The police were putting out a considerable number of press releases and public appeals that year and it would appear not everyone had heard what McPhee had said. Certainly, Tommy Hogg must have missed this information because he was still giving interviews to the media about this man many years later and garnering quite a bit of air time and column inches.

Right from the start, I'd never been a fan of the theory that said this suspicious-looking man could have been the killer. Gut instinct was telling me that he could not be the murderer. Back in my undercover days, when I posed as a contract killer and I'd plot and plan murder with some aggrieved wife or businessman, I would never have dreamt of suggesting that I would catch a bus to carry out a killing. Too many potential witnesses, too high a risk of being captured on CCTV, and how the heck are you going to escape the scene, by hailing down a bus? I don't think so somehow.

Talking of CCTV, I'm sure we have all seen examples of when CCTV footage has provided vital evidence which has gone a long way towards solving a major crime. In June 2002, The Highland Council agreed additional funding of £60,000 to sustain the development of CCTV in Highland towns, one of which was Nairn.

Nairn's system of cameras relayed images to the local police station. The system wasn't as exhaustive as some found in our inner cities, but nonetheless it did exist. In February 2004, the Resources Committee of the Highland Council agreed to accept a tender that would see the refurbishment of this system, followed by a five-year maintenance contract. Therefore, on the night of Alistair Wilson's murder, Nairn's CCTV system should have been fully up and running without fault.

One of Nairn's cameras was positioned high up on a church wall on King Street (the A96), at the junction with Crescent Road. It was a large dome camera and should have provided images that would have seen down Crescent Road, probably as far as the vicinity of Alistair's house. Astonishingly, this camera was not working on the night of the murder. This has provided plenty of fuel for the conspiracy theorists out there, but I was more concerned in finding out whose responsibility it had been to ensure the camera was working properly.

I get incensed when systems that should be working aren't, especially those run by public bodies. Other unsolved murders I've researched have been hampered by the fact that CCTV systems that should have been working were not. In two cases, systems on a train station and a bus were faulty and the outcomes of those investigations might have been very different, had images been provided. Justice was either delayed or denied and frankly, that isn't good enough. I would like to see legislation brought in that places a legal obligation on public bodies to maintain their systems properly, with individuals held to account if they fail in their duty.

Sometimes a negative sighting of a suspect on a CCTV trawl can be just as helpful as a positive sighting of a suspect. If you identify a location where you know a suspect definitely didn't appear, then you can discount that location or route of travel and focus your resources elsewhere. Adopting a process of elimination, you can sometimes work out where a suspect must have been or travelled, because other possible areas are all discounted and you can work from there. Of course in Alistair Wilson's case because of the unforgivable negligence, rank incompetence or some other unacceptable oversight or omission, no such CCTV evidence was forthcoming from the camera at the end of Crescent Road. As I write this, I can feel my blood pressure rising because it is not beyond the realms of possibility that this camera would have captured images of the gunman, justice could then have been dealt out and I wouldn't be writing this book.

In 2017, I contacted The Highland Council. I wanted to know whose fault it was that this camera was not working properly. Were the council responsible, might a CCTV company be to blame, or was it the police's fault? Miles Watters, freedom of information and data protection manager, wrote: 'Given the above [he sent me some links to council documents] and my own knowledge, I don't believe that there has ever been a member of Council staff with responsibility for managing the CCTV in Nairn and I believe that in November 2004, the responsibility for the management would have lain with the Police and not the Council'.

I hope somebody who was working for the Northern Constabulary in 2004 is reading this and hanging their head in shame.

While police efforts to find witnesses or CCTV footage of the gunman from elsewhere were not reaping rewards, it didn't take long for the police to discover what type of firearm was used to kill Alistair Wilson. The fatal bullets would have been recovered from his body during the post-mortem, or from the scene of the crime if they had passed clean through him. Once retrieved, these bullets would give a solid indication of the weapon used to fire them – the smaller the bullet, the smaller the type of gun used to fire them. The police went public early on in the investigation, saying that the weapon was a small handgun.

Soon afterwards, the police told the media and the public that there had been a 'very significant' breakthrough. On 8 December 2004, ten days after the shooting, workmen from the local council were clearing out drains in Seabank Road, Nairn. As part of this process, drain covers were removed from the roadside gutters and the gullies beneath cleared of debris. While doing this, one of the workmen discovered a small handgun at the bottom of a gulley. The police were notified, roads were sealed off and some of the detectives on the inquiry became somewhat optimistic.

A local journalist tried in vain to get an interview with the workman who had found the gun. He wanted a 'How did you feel when you saw the gun?' sort of story, but the council had already warned their employees to remain firmly tight-lipped.

The gun was a small semi-automatic pistol. 'Semi-automatic' means it can fire either a single shot or fire bullets in a short burst if the trigger is pulled back and held. The magazine, which fits into the handle of the gun, can hold six bullets, or 'rounds' as they are often called. That is all – this is not the type of weapon to take to a gunfight. The gun was manufactured between 1922 and 1945 by a company called Haenel in Suhl, Germany. It had been designed and patented by Hugo Schmeisser, whose name later became synonymous with the MP18, the world's first machine gun that he invented. About 40,000 of these tiny handguns had been manufactured and this particular murder weapon did have a serial number, although inquiries revealed that it had never been officially registered in the UK.

The gun was about four-and-a-half inches long, weighed around 400 g and went by a number of different names: Pocket pistol, Handbag gun, Waistcoat gun, Ladies' gun and more. Of course the ammunition it fired was equally diminutive: .25 calibre. When compared to the more commonplace 9mm ammunition of today, this gives you an idea of why that type of gun has gone out of fashion and is not usually used by assassins, gangsters or law enforcement officers today.

The bullets that killed Alistair Wilson were manufactured between 1983 and 1993 by a company called Sellier & Bellot, who were based in Vlasim, in the Czech Republic. They are still in business today.

In 2005, detectives travelled far and wide in their efforts to gather more evidence about the gun and its ammunition. There was a theory that the gun could have been brought into the UK after the Second World War, perhaps smuggled in by a returning soldier who had nabbed himself a trophy. Other theories abounded, including one that I thought had some merit, namely that the gun might have originated from the Channel Isles, which were occupied by the Nazis during World War II. This gun was described to me as the type that would be presented to a Nazi officer on graduation from training, so maybe it had been discarded after the Occupation ended in 1945.

In the early stages of the investigation the police reached out to serving and former military personnel to see if they could help with the past history of the gun. Details were posted on the Ministry of Defence Oracle website, which attracted over 1.5 million visits a month. The police emphasised how rarely this type of weapon was found in the UK, but all their efforts to trace its full history, criminal or otherwise, appeared to be floundering.

The weapon was sent for forensic examination and was soon confirmed by scientists as the gun that was used to kill Alistair Wilson. There were no fingerprints on it. Not surprising perhaps, because it might have lain in that drain for ten days, with Highland winter weather washing any such prints away. It could have been an entirely different story, had the police set their initial search parameters wider the day after the murder. Senior officers always have to set parameters, I appreciate that. They will pose questions to themselves like, over what range do we deploy search teams? Over what areas do we conduct house-to-house inquiries? How wide do we set the parameters of our CCTV trawl? And I fully accept that sometimes resources are limited and officers cannot be everywhere. However, in this case search teams were delegated to the beaches, which are about 500 metres from the scene of the murder, when anybody with local knowledge would have told you in a heartbeat (and indeed I was by a local journalist) that the tides were so low, an escape by boat would have been impossible.

The police told the public very early on in the investigation that they were looking in gardens, rubbish bins and drains in the vicinity of the murder, but clearly did not focus on a large enough area. Seabank Road is only about 600 metres from the murder scene. If the gun was discarded in that drain by the gunman as he escaped the scene of the crime on that fateful Sunday night (as opposed to ditching it there at some later date), then the police failure to spread the search net wider, and therefore retrieve the gun early on in the inquiry, before the weather washed vital evidence away, might be an error of such serious magnitude that the killer may now remain free because of it.

Of course the killer may have been very forensically aware, and may have exercised extreme caution when handling the gun, thereby ensuring there was no forensic evidence to retrieve in any event, but that would require a greater degree of forensic awareness than you might glean from watching a few episodes of *CSI*. Police financial resources are not limitless, so when a firearm is submitted for forensic examination, the police may initially ask that only certain parts of the gun are examined in the first instance – forensic examinations do not come cheap. The police will invariably request that the obvious areas of a gun are tested for DNA traces; areas like the handle, the trigger and the trigger guard. It may only be later that the police may ask for the inside of a magazine to be tested, and that request may only be made if the search of the areas previously tested comes back as negative.

The area of a semi-automatic pistol that sometimes yields DNA results is the underneath of the barrel at the handle end. This is because that part of the gun slides back and forth rapidly each time the gun is fired, sometimes picking up DNA from the space between the thumb and forefinger of the shooter. If a gunman then hurriedly cleans the weapon as so often see in the movies, he will not be able to clean the underneath of the barrel thoroughly without dismantling the gun or holding the barrel back, for the underneath of the barrel returns to the non-firing position where it cannot be easily accessed. I would sincerely hope that the gun that killed Alistair Wilson has been fully and thoroughly tested over the years, including the magazine and any unfired bullets that may have been found in it.

There has never been any indication from Veronica Wilson as to whether the man at her door was wearing gloves or not.

It must have been a crushing blow for the detectives when they were later told that a full DNA profile could not be retrieved from the gun. Once again, was this due to the inclement weather, or was it because of the expert handling of the weapon by the gunman? DNA science continues to gallop forward at an astonishing rate. Over the years the gun has been repeatedly examined, apparently in an effort to detect the minutest trace of DNA, which could then be developed into a fuller profile. I'm sure this will continue in the future.

The location of this gun is hugely significant, and while greater minds than mine will comment upon it later in the book, I'll give you my thoughts now. Veronica Wilson says she saw the gunman disappearing to her left, down Crescent Road. That would be towards The Shambles Bar, Marine Road and The Links. For a moment, let's work on the theory there was a car waiting for the gunman nearby. If he got into such a car, then it is a short drive, of only a minute or two, to Seabank Road. The most straightforward route would be along Marine Road, a left turn into Seafield Street, then Seabank Road is the fourth turning on the left. The drain where the gun was found was towards the end of Seabank Road, near the junction with Academy Street, the main A96.

If the gunman was picked up by a driver and got in the front passenger seat and his driver then took the route I've described, then once the car had arrived in Seabank Road, all the gunman would have to do was open the passenger door slightly and drop the gun into the drain, because it would have been on the passenger side. I would argue this would not make the car particularly noticeable and is a low-risk thing to do.

If the gunman drove himself away from Crescent Road and took the same route, he would have had to bring the car to a complete standstill, get out, walk around the front or the rear of the car, and then walk a couple of paces to the drain before dropping the gun. This would all increase the possibility of being spotted. I therefore believe there is a distinct possibility that an accomplice – a getaway driver, if you will – may have been lying in wait nearby.

Let's ignore any getaway car and explore the possibility that the gunman travelled on foot to Seabank Road. There is no direct route by foot that would keep you away from residential roads; there isn't an alleyway all the way, nor some field that he might have traversed. At some point he would have had to walk down a residential road, all of which would have increased the risk of being seen. It's not out of the question, of course, and 7.20 p.m. or thereabouts on a Sunday night is probably as good a time as any not to get spotted, but with the adrenaline pumping, and a desperate desire to move around unnoticed, I'm not convinced the gunman travelled from Crescent Road to Seabank Road by foot, immediately after shooting Alistair Wilson. If he did, where did he go to next? A left turn into Academy Road would take him towards the area he'd just come from, the part of Nairn with CCTV cameras (some of which were working!), the bus stop and other, more heavily populated streets.

Did the gunman actually deposit the gun in that drain on the evening of the crime, or did he ditch the murder weapon there at some later stage? That would be an incredibly high-risk thing to do because it would mean the gun was either in his possession, or somehow under his control until he abandoned it, thereby increasing the risk of being captured with it. Maybe he handed the gun to someone else, who thoroughly cleaned it for him and then got rid of it. The possibilities are almost endless, but my favourite theory is that he had a getaway driver nearby. He ditched the gun as I described and then they turned right on to the A96 towards Inverness and away to freedom.

Of course I could be wrong, let's just hope we all find out one day.

On the night of the murder, as soon as they possibly could, the police threw up roadblocks around Nairn and checked traffic heading for Inverness. I strongly suspect the suspect had well and truly flown the nest by the time that happened.

On 1 November 2005, almost a year after the murder, DCI McPhee led a press conference for the numerous media outlets that had gathered eagerly to hear the latest on the investigation. A tape of the 999 call made by Veronica Wilson was played. In an unabashed effort to tug on the heartstrings of anybody who might know something about the crime, footage was also shown of the moment Veronica and Alistair Wilson's four-year-old son was told by a child psychologist that his daddy was dead. Parts of these recordings were made available to the BBC and Grampian TV, who were making documentaries that would later be shown in Scotland.

In this video footage the psychologist, Helen Kenward, asks the four-year-old what he thinks has happened to his dad. The boy replies, 'Still in the hospital and… and… I think he's OK.' The psychologist later says, 'Well, Daddy's not going to come back.' 'Why?' asks the boy, and the psychologist replies, 'Because the shot made him dead.' I have seen this footage, and whilst the boy's identity and facial reactions are kept hidden from the audience, his youthful, tender and softly spoken voice is clearly audible, and provides a haunting and stark insight into the realities, the impact and the devastation of Alistair Wilson's murder.

CHAPTER FOUR

WRONGFUL ACCUSATIONS

Murder has featured heavily in my life. As a young detective, I investigated murders; in fact, I never worked on a case we couldn't solve. In my undercover days I pretended to be a cold-blooded killer on a number of occasions, which meant I plotted and planned murder with a variety of people who all had one thing in common: they wanted me to kill someone. And I was the intended victim of a murder plot, a plot hatched by some very serious criminals with connections to terrorism, who wanted to wipe me from the face of the earth. Their plan was so advanced and the threat so real, I had to abandon my identity and my home and move into the witness protection programme. Every day, the threat of assassination loomed over me.

I know a bit about murder.

Back in the 1980s when I was investigating murders, the tools at our disposal bore little resemblance to the wide array of investigative techniques and tactics available to modern-day detectives. There was no such thing as DNA analysis back then, no CCTV to call upon, while smartphone evidence that could place a person at a given location at a given time was still to be invented. Yet we solved the same percentage of murders back then as the police do today. In fact, as murder rates have increased recently, especially in London, detection rates have dropped. Upon my retirement from the police way back in 1999, I was puzzled and troubled that so many people were still committing murder in the twenty-first century and getting away with it. How could that be so? I decided to try and find some answers. I've discovered a few, but I'm still searching for many, many more.

The year 2005 was all about unsolved murders for me, as it was for the detectives on the Alistair Wilson inquiry. I spent most of that year travelling the length and breadth of the UK, researching and writing about a variety of cases for a book that was to be published towards the end of the year. I considered including Alistair Wilson's case in that book, but to be frank, I was sure the police were going to solve it, so it didn't feature among the cases I selected.

That year I spent a lot of time away from my wife and two sons, then aged three and four. Sarah was OK about this as she knew I was striving to forge a new career for myself, post police. And besides, if I'm on the case of those who've committed murder and got away with it, then my amazing wife is always fully behind me. I'd been given an advance by my publisher, but had spent the vast majority of it on travel, accommodation and other expenses. Then, as now, I was not in it for the money.

What I discovered in 2005 and beyond is that there is substantial evidence to show that if a murderer is not caught after their first killing, they may well go on to slaughter again. Too many killers roam free among us in our towns, villages and cities. I hope you've grasped what motivates me by now.

In the world of psychology there is a widespread acceptance that stress or anxiety can affect a person's ability to recall events. Various studies have reached conflicting conclusions: some say anxiety has a positive effect, while others have found the opposite, that anxiety can make people less able to recall events accurately. In extreme cases witnessing a particularly horrifying event can trigger Post-traumatic Stress Disorder (PTSD), but I'm glad to report, I have found no evidence of Veronica developing that condition.

Stress or anxiety can trigger the flight-or-fight response in individuals, depending on the release of chemicals within the brain. What I think is beyond doubt or debate is that Veronica suffered extreme shock when she found her husband fatally wounded on their doorstep. Her responses to that and her subsequent actions must all be looked at in this context. I do remain concerned though that an image of the gunman, whether compiled by an artist or via computer imagery, has never been released to the public. It has been common practice in other similar and notorious cases. Together with many others I still ask the question, 'Why not in this case?'

It would appear that Veronica was keen to do all she could to help the investigation. She voluntarily underwent a hypnosis-style treatment called regressive cognitive therapy in an effort to try and elicit any information that might lay hidden, but unfortunately, this process did not bear fruit.

I saw Veronica during my 2005 trip, not to speak to, but I passed her in the street. My sympathies went out to her then, as they do now. My wife and I have been fortunate enough to raise our two boys together. Quite how Veronica has managed as a single parent, I don't know.

In all of my visits to Nairn, whether in 2005, 2009, 2017, 2018, or any of the years in between, I have heard gossip, rumours and theories in which Veronica Wilson's name is repeatedly mentioned, often with an air of suspicion surrounding her. If you are one of the 'Veronica is involved' brigade, let me remind you of what DCI McPhee said on 1 November 2005, by which time the police had had almost a year to ponder over every single aspect of her life: 'It would be reasonable for most folk to expect us to look at whether Veronica Wilson was involved somehow and we did. But I can say we have investigated the immediate Wilson family and the extended family of Veronica very closely and there is no evidence at all to implicate any of them either directly or indirectly with Alistair's death.'

DCI McPhee could not have been clearer or more unequivocal in my opinion. Yet his words have done little over the years to silence the rumour mill. I have long hoped to spend some considerable time with Veronica Wilson and I told the police that if I did, then I felt this book could go a long way towards slaying the dragon of gossip and rumour. But it was not to be.

Not a shred of evidence has ever been produced to implicate Veronica in any way, yet still the rumours persist to this day. The harsh and yet very stark reality is that there is at least one retired police officer who is still spreading rumours around town about Veronica's 'involvement'. Part of the reason for this continual and poisonous rumour-mongering is because only Veronica and Alistair saw the gunman on their doorstep in Crescent Road. Unfortunately, for all involved, there is no other independent witness to the events on the Wilson doorstep, who can verify what Veronica says about the man who clearly wielded the gun. It is therefore her account of events on the night of Sunday, 28 November 2004 upon which we rely.

To all the doubters out there, I say this: if you had been involved in any sort of crime, would you allow yourself to undergo a hypnosis-style treatment in an effort to extract deep and hidden information from you? I certainly wouldn't. Would you, on a number of occasions since the killing, voluntarily put yourself in front of the media, knowing your every word will be pored over, examined in the minutest detail, and of course compared to your previous appearances?

As you've probably guessed by now, Veronica Wilson has my sympathy. To lose your husband and the father of your two young children is tragic, no matter what the circumstances. To witness what she did that night must have been deeply traumatising. If only someone else had seen what happened.

CHAPTER FIVE

LIFE AFTER SO10

I returned home in December 2005 with Alistair Wilson's murder occupying a lot of headspace. Visiting the scene of the crime, the location where the gun was found and speaking to as many people affected by the crime as we did had left an indelible mark on me. Much as I wanted to dedicate my time solely to researching Alistair's murder, the harsh reality was that I urgently needed to bring some cash into our bank account in order to support my family.

Since leaving the police in 1999, I had done alright. My autobiography, *The Gangbuster*, had been published and as a result, my name entered the public domain. Instead of living a highly secretive life, I could now be easily found by news outlets who wanted me to comment on crime and policing. In 2002 I was approached by a television production company, Tiger Aspect, to see if I'd be willing to work as the story consultant to a TV drama, *Murphy's Law*, starring James

Nesbitt of *Cold Feet* fame and more. Two six-part series of *Murphy's Law* had already aired, but both the BBC and Tiger Aspect wanted to breathe new life into the show and take it in a direction it had not travelled before. I was about to enter a world so completely different to the one I previously knew.

I was called to a meeting in a restaurant in Soho, London. On announcing myself to the maître d', I was ushered upstairs, where a group of about ten people sat around a large oval table with one spare seat. A woman stood up and introduced herself to me as the producer of the show. She welcomed me warmly and went around the table introducing writers, directors, executives and more. I couldn't keep tally of them all. After the handshakes and greetings, I sat down. Almost immediately, the woman sitting next to me on my right piped up rather caustically, 'Have you actually read your book?' She was clearly alluding to the fact that I'd co-written *The Gangbuster* with an experienced journalist and frankly, she was taking the mickey. My retort was swift, 'I wouldn't read that shit if you paid me. Now, shall we move on?'

The ice was broken and I went on to explain what life undercover was really like, rather than the cartoon caricature image portrayed in their previous two series when James Nesbitt had played a different and sometimes less-than-believable role each week. The large and uncompromising dose of the realities of working undercover that I gave them obviously worked: I was hired. I had a great time teaching James, the writers and the production team about undercover policing. At times I'd scare the life out of them all, most notably in a pub one night when the lead character Jimmy was in the bathroom. He'd made the mistake of standing with his back to the bathroom door. Working undercover, you've always got to know where the escape routes are, wherever you might be, and the areas where danger may spring from. There was Jimmy, having a leak, blissfully switched off from potential threat. Stealthily, I crept up behind him, put my arm around his neck and told him how in real life he could now be dead. Being the consummate professional and frankly brilliant actor that he is, James took it all on board and thereafter delivered a true tour de force in the Jimmy Murphy role. A grittier, darker and more realistic show was the result of all our efforts.

We went on to make three more series before the show was eventually decommissioned. The last series we made was nominated in the Best Drama category of the BAFTA Awards. The producer described me in the media as the 'inspiration' for the show and it remains a piece of work that I am hugely proud of.

But by the time 2006 came around, *Murphy's Law* was no more and book sales had tailed off significantly. A former colleague, with whom I had worked back in the late 1970s, who had left the police to forge a highly successful career in the world of private investigations and security, was pestering me to go and work for her. She kept badgering me to go and do some 'proper work' instead of floundering around in the make-believe world of TV. I'd resisted that call because I thought working for private clients would not hold any attraction and that the cases would be petty, trifling matters. After dealing with some of the highest echelons of serious and organised crime in the police anything else was surely going to be a bit of an anticlimax. Oh well, needs must.

The first major case I worked on was one of blackmail. A flamboyant and well-connected gay man, who I will call Juan, was blackmailing a wealthy, married family man, who I will call Richard. These two men had had a passionate, albeit short-lived fling, unbeknown to Richard's wife, who was convinced her husband was 100 per cent heterosexual. Richard had lavished expensive gifts and treats upon Juan, but once he discovered his lover was HIV-positive, he ended the relationship. After the break-up, Juan repeatedly threatened to expose the secret to one and all, unless Richard paid him an eye-watering sum of money. Richard could have gone to the police – blackmail is blackmail regardless of the circumstances leading up to it – but he did not want to run the risk of public exposure through police involvement and a potential court case. Not to mention the inevitable resulting fallout, should his unsuspecting wife find out.

Richard was wealthy enough to hire the services of private investigators and believe you me, they do not come cheap. Does this mean that the private security industry often acts as a private police service for the rich and powerful? I'm afraid to say it does. If you have the means then you can hire experts in their field, former police and military who will basically cocoon and protect you from all the dangers the world has to offer. And if by chance someone does happen to wrong you, then some of the best detective minds that the police have ever employed will be yours to investigate, bug, hack, blag and infiltrate as you see fit. That does not sit comfortably with me, but at that time in my life with my wife on a career break and three sons to support, including my eldest, who was about to start at university, I desperately needed to earn some money. Did I sell my soul to the highest bidder? Arguably, I did.

We started off by doing conventional surveillance on Juan. I was the new face on the team, but the other operatives learnt from day one that I was vastly experienced in covert surveillance. The intelligence we gathered on Juan was all fed back to those employing us, who in turn were liaising directly with Richard.

Juan was drinking virtually every day in a gay bar in London. Me and a colleague would go into this bar, get a drink and keep a close eye on him. He was very well known in there and appeared to have a large circle of associates. We watched, we overheard, and we catalogued the intelligence. The office was also carrying out its own inquiries and we were told what they wanted us to know. One thing they did tell us was that Juan was claiming unemployment benefits.

After a while we discovered that Juan was using his home as an art studio, where he was creating a collection of paintings for an upcoming exhibition in a local gallery. We saw him make what looked to be deals to sell paintings so we set the office to work on his tax affairs. Was he declaring this income? Of course not, he was on the dole.

The operation was moving forwards, but not at the pace the office demanded. It was costing Richard thousands of pounds and Juan was still making the blackmail demands which he couldn't put off forever. So I came up with an idea: why didn't I go undercover in this gay bar, befriend Juan and get some concrete evidence about him working while claiming unemployment benefit and failing to declare his income to the tax authorities? I might possibly get some evidence of drug taking because Juan did seem to visit the bathroom far more frequently than the average customer. Undercover operations in the police are often very cost-effective and I thought this case could follow suit.

Working on *Murphy's Law*, I'd read dozens of scripts from many, many writers, and I was beginning to harbour dreams that I could one day pen drama of my own. I learnt about story, plot, character and structure, and felt comfortable that I could pose as a writer. But I wasn't going to pretend to be gay, because that could have got me in all sorts of awkward situations. Instead, I was to pose as a straight writer developing a TV series about a young man's journey through discovering his own sexuality.

My plan was agreed and sanctioned by the office, so, deep breath, pen and notebook at the ready, into the gay bar I ventured, although this time it was not as an invisible grey man of surveillance, but in a role and I wanted to be noticed.

Word soon got round about my 'project'. I had men literally queuing to tell me stories of their sexuality. I've always thought myself a liberally minded man of the world, but I soon realised how little I knew. Some of these stories were harrowing and involved abuse and mistreatment, others made me blush. Juan's outgoing personality meant that he told all and we got on rather well.

It didn't take long before he was offering me paintings to buy and inviting me to his exhibition. He told me how well he'd been doing selling his work and how much money he'd earned. I suppose it was greed that made him resort to blackmail, tax evasion and fraudulent claims of unemployment benefit. Shame really, he was clearly very talented.

After spending a few days in the bar listening to Juan's life story, I visited the gallery and bought one of his paintings, using money supplied by the client. Juan had asked that I pay him in cash, which I did. Our surveillance team followed Juan and later saw him bank some of the money. This was all good evidence.

As I have said, Juan did use the bathroom a lot and gathering by his demeanour, he was obviously on something. In my previous life, many years ago, I would probably have been interested in the drugs side of things, but the evidence I was gathering was predominantly based around Juan's fraudulent activity and that's where my focus was concentrated.

The office was satisfied that we'd gathered enough evidence against Juan. His blackmail demands showed no sign of abating, so it was decided that the time to act was upon us. My colleagues kept Juan under surveillance one sunny afternoon, with the boss tagging on to the end of the surveillance convoy. Juan decided to enjoy a takeaway coffee and read the newspaper on a park bench. While the surveillance operatives kept watch, snapping away on their hidden cameras, the boss approached with a dossier under his arm. He sidled up next to Juan, introduced himself and began to unravel the stream of evidence that we had accumulated against him.

Juan was given an ultimatum: either he ceased his blackmail demands immediately and for ever, or the appropriate authorities would be made aware of his working while claiming unemployment benefit and his failure to declare the income from his paintings. The choice was his.

Unsurprisingly, he promised to stop blackmailing Richard immediately. He signed a written agreement to that effect and Richard never heard another word from him.

So, there you have it, a glittering example of 'justice' within the private security industry. Is it satisfactory, were the public and society best served by all these shenanigans? Of course not, but the wealthy client got what he wanted and we all got paid. I wasn't particularly happy and didn't have a great sense of job satisfaction, but at least it kept the wolf from my family's door.

My undercover and surveillance work had been well received by the boss and he was keen for me to get my Security Industry Authority (SIA), Close Protection (CP) licence. This would mean that I could act as a bodyguard to the rich and famous, as a door supervisor at any establishment that needed security, and, if so minded, I could act as a team leader or even a humble security guard. How the mighty fall, I thought to myself. Not so long ago I was travelling the world at the top of my game as a globally renowned undercover detective, now I was to be a bodyguard. Then I remembered I had hungry mouths to feed so I went on a four-week course which cost thousands of pounds, but I sailed through. Training alongside me were some knuckle-dragging boneheads I wouldn't have trusted to look after my kids' goldfish. Others were former police and military, who would have ensured anyone, anywhere, could rest safe in the knowledge they were brilliantly protected. The money I spent turned out to be a very sound investment for I didn't have long to wait before the phone rang.

A Russian billionaire, who had made his fortune after the

collapse of the Soviet Union and the introduction of free market economies into Russia, went missing in suspicious circumstances. He had a two-year-old son, on whom he doted. This son and his mother were living in a luxury flat in London at the time of the disappearance. Business associates and lawyers moved swiftly to protect the boy, for it was he who would inherit the earth, should his billionaire father be gone forever.

A security team was despatched to central London to carry out round-the-clock protective surveillance on the boy, who I will call Alex, and his mother. I got the call and made my way.

I hate protective surveillance: it falls between two stalls and is notoriously difficult to do. It's not the type of traditional surveillance you would carry out on a suspect, where your brief is to follow from an appropriate distance and remain covert at all times. And it's not traditional close protection, where the person you are protecting (the principal) knows you are there so you can stay very close to them and can therefore plot and plan their movements. It's neither one, nor the other. We were being asked to protect Alex and his mum without them knowing we were there. We didn't know what their movements were going to be, we couldn't be inside their home and we had to remain hidden while being close enough to protect them if anything untoward happened. It was a virtually impossible task.

So, we carried out this protective surveillance over a frustrating weekend. We followed Alex and his mum to the shops and the park. The tensions among the team were high. The risk of potential threat appeared to be very real, judging by what had happened to the dad and by the amount of resources being thrown at this task. All the time we kept reporting back to the office how unsatisfactory we thought this protective surveillance situation was. If we were really going to keep this two-year-old boy and his mum safe from any possible risk then we needed to be running their lives and we needed to be all over them, not pretending we were dog walkers, tourists, joggers or lovers enjoying a central London park.

The office listened, so too did the clients. Alex's mum was told to expect us and we swung into full-on close protection mode. Now we all knew what our roles were. This was what the team had experience in and were trained to do. Three of us went into the flat and met Alex and his mum. While our team leader briefed the mum on what life with twenty-four-hour close protection was going to be like, another team member did a full reconnaissance of the flat. As a highly trained and well-paid bodyguard I did what I thought was right, I got down on the floor and played trains with Alex, who was only two or three years younger than my own boys. I immediately warmed to him and was in my element.

A Norland nanny and a personal assistant were hired for Alex and his mum. These very costly members of the team were deemed necessary in order that the mother could still enjoy a life of her own. I make no further comment. The flat was deemed unsuitable for keeping Alex and his mum safe from whatever threat the world might have in store for them, so an extremely desirable London house was arranged. State-of-the-art security systems were installed under my supervision. Living in the witness protection programme had given me a very good grounding in what was needed. A fleet of appropriate vehicles were sourced. No expense was spared in keeping Alex safe.

Alex was a delightful, bright, engaging little boy. He possessed a charm that for many was impossible to resist. However, I did not fall into that trap. He and I got on brilliantly, but I was to spend so much time with him over the next two years or so that I felt it important that I exerted the same discipline over him as I did my own children. I wasn't going to be some sort of surrogate father, I was merely doing what I thought was right for the child. Members of the team who did not have children would sometimes indulge him and let him get away with stuff. But I didn't and Alex knew that. We both knew exactly where we stood, the boundaries were clear and so we developed a close bond. The hugely talented nanny was grateful that she and I sang from the same song sheet.

Being a part of the lives of people with access to vast wealth was an eye-opener for me, an ex-copper from South London. I didn't particularly enjoy the incessant shopping trips to Harrods or Harvey Nichols, nor the endless hours spent in the best restaurants in town. Neither did Alex. I loved our trips to the park, or the zoo, even though I was always doing my job and constantly looking out for any potential threat.

Alex's mum loved a holiday, so we travelled the world, often experiencing the billionaire lifestyle as we went. We flew in private jets, stayed in the most amazing houses and resorts and enjoyed some incredible food. I had my first experience of lobster – very nice it was too! I spent countless hours in the swimming pool with Alex, teaching him how to swim, as well as splashing about mischievously and having a fabulous time. It was great to have a regular wage for the first time in a long while.

Through no fault of his mum or anyone else, Alex had not developed a social circle of friends his own age, so one day I suggested to the bosses that he should meet my two youngest boys. Both the bosses and Alex's mum agreed. On a day trip to the coast my family came as well. Alex and my boys got on famously; he loved having slightly older playmates, whom he charmed and entertained in his own inimitable way. They were inseparable that day. Other days together followed, including a memorable barbeque at my house. Quite what the neighbours thought as an entourage of blacked-out vehicles, bodyguards, staff and little Alex descended on our modest three-bedroom home I'm not quite sure, but we all had a wonderfully sober time – a rarity for a barbeque of mine!

But it was not all fun and frolics. One weekend we received intelligence that a private jet had landed at an airport near London. This aircraft apparently carried a bunch of people determined to wrestle Alex from our grasp and smuggle him out of the country. We immediately abandoned the house that we guarded day and night and spirited everyone away to a safe location. The plot was thwarted and a clear message went out that we were more than capable of doing what we were paid to do.

While the money was nice, it did mean in the early stages of our task that I was seeing a lot more of Alex than my own kids. My boys were less than impressed when I told them I was going to be out of the country with Alex one Christmas.

But the time away from my family working very long hours was worth it, because at the end of the task we could afford to extend our house by another bedroom and bathroom. Happy wife equals happy life.

The writing was on the wall. After two years of being protected by us, Alex's mum made it clear she was keen to leave the UK and make her home abroad. It was time to look for employment elsewhere.

Towards the end of our stint protecting Alex we'd operated a four-days-on, four-days-off system. We'd also been alternating day and night shifts. This had given me time to continue with drama consultancy work as it arose and pursue my ambition of writing some drama of my own. However, thoughts of Alistair and Veronica Wilson and their boys would not go away. I continued to monitor any media reports on Alistair's murder, but these in the main had only really surfaced as each anniversary of the killing loomed. Towards the end of 2009, I made a determined effort to get some publicity for the case. I approached a TV production company I'd got to know through providing bits of security for them when they door-stepped potentially violent people, those whose wrongdoing they went on to expose in their documentaries. Channel 4 were commissioning a series of low-budget twenty-four-minute documentaries called *First Cut*, which were ideal for young up-and-coming filmmakers.

The production company introduced me to a youthful, enthusiastic and determined producer/director called Tom Randall. I briefed him fully on Alistair Wilson's murder and Channel 4 gave us some development cash to cover our expenses. We were told to go and uncover all that we possibly could. I was delighted – even a low-budget documentary that would be broadcasted nationally could only help in discovering the truth, I thought.

We were soon heading for Nairn.

CHAPTER SIX

BACK ON THE CASE

I thought I'd make the Northern Constabulary aware of our trip to Nairn and our intentions so I emailed them, asking for an interview with one of the officers involved in the case. DCI McPhee had retired from the police, but I was hoping they would put another senior officer up for interview, one who now had responsibility for the investigation. Their response shocked me. Duncan McKenzie, the Northern Constabulary's senior media relations officer, wrote back: 'There is currently no inquiry team as such.'

So, there it was in black and white: less than five years after Alistair Wilson's murder, the police were no longer investigating this crime. Had they really explored every possible snippet of information, every scrap of intelligence, every theory and rumour so exhaustively that they'd decided there was nothing more they could do? They must have thought they had. I told Tom Randall that it looked as though we were the only people currently investigating this crime.

The Northern Constabulary's website stated: 'At this time there appears to be no motive for the murder'. It looked like they'd given up trying to find one. Not long after the shooting, the charity Crimestoppers had put up a £10,000 reward for information that would lead to the crime being solved. That reward was no longer up for grabs. If a relative of mine had been slaughtered in similar circumstances and this was the current state of play, I would be distinctly unimpressed.

All of this merely spurred me and Tom on. Once we'd dumped our kit in our bed-and-breakfast, which was next door to Alistair Wilson's house, we set about our work. The first person we interviewed was a local journalist who had lived in Nairn all his life and was one of the first scribes to arrive at the scene on the night of the murder. His knowledge of Nairn was almost without equal and he spoke of the tremendous shock the crime had caused in the town, a place entirely unused to any sort of serious crime. He told us how TV trucks and vans had lined nearby Cumming Street as the case garnered worldwide media attention in the days following the shooting. He expressed disappointment that 'The case is going nowhere'.

While loath to criticise the police, he said considerable resources had been ploughed into the investigation and he felt that on the surface it appeared they had left 'no stone unturned'. He had spoken to DCI McPhee a number of times and he felt McPhee had been passionate, thorough and that he'd cooperated with the media. But this seasoned and vastly experienced journo did feel it was time for a change of strategy by the police and that they should now reveal the information surrounding the envelope. Tom and I were in strong agreement. We discussed how the lack of information from the police about the envelope and the discussions surrounding it between Alistair and Veronica Wilson had created a void filled with gossip and rumour. The journalist told me that some people even question whether the envelope ever existed.

Though keen to emphasise that he was not a detective, he did offer some personal views on the killer. He didn't think the killer was a professional hitman and went on to explain: 'The gun he used was not very efficient and had to be used at very close range. He revealed himself to Veronica and dumped the gun nearby.' He also declared confidential police sources had told him that they didn't think the gunman was a professional hitman either.

Before we left this highly respected man of considerable local standing, he wanted to give us some idea of the scale of the police investigation. He said they'd taken many hundreds of statements and collected over a thousand DNA samples. He told how exactly one week after the crime, the police had stopped hundreds of cars and spoken to the occupants. But the police's inability to catch the killer gave rise to a remaining nagging fear in the minds of locals: 'A murderer could be in our midst'.

By now it was late so we gave our thanks and said farewell. We grabbed a bite to eat and headed to our beds.

The following morning, Tom and I headed to Inverness, the capital city of the Highlands. About fifteen miles from Nairn, it's virtually a straight drive along the A96. The administrative centre for the region, in 2004, it had a population of some

60,000. It is, of course, where Alistair Wilson worked for the Bank of Scotland.

My first port of call was the planning department of the local council, as I heard there had been some dispute between Alistair and Andy Burnett, landlord of The Havelock, which as you will remember was opposite Alistair's house. The delightful staff were very welcoming and extremely helpful. I was given unfettered access to their files.

I discovered that on 8 November 2004, just twenty days before Alistair Wilson was shot, Andy Burnett submitted a planning application to the council for some external decking, which was to eat up some of the space previously used for car parking. Burnett had already built this decking, unaware that he needed planning permission, so the application was in fact a retrospective one.

Alistair was not at all happy about this and laid out his objections to the council in a letter dated 23 November. He wrote, 'I write to formally object to the planning application. Firstly, there appears no recognition that this is in effect a retrospective application as the "decking" in the car park was constructed in May this year. It is with the benefit of the experience of living with a beer garden outside my front door that I raise the following points.'

He went on to complain forcibly about a number of matters, among them:

- The decking had been used for the serving of food and drink whenever the pub was open. This had apparently included late nights, with the bar doors open and consequent noise and disturbance.

- He stated that on a regular basis he had found glasses in his garden and broken glass strewn in the street.
- During the summer months, he and his family felt uncomfortable using their front door and looking out of their front windows because customers would frequently look back at them.
- The decking had used up car parking space, which now meant there was increased traffic volumes parking in Crescent Road, and sometimes the Wilsons' driveway had been blocked.

Alistair's penultimate line of his letter read: 'Crescent Road is predominantly a residential area with several families with young children and I feel this objection is in the best interests of all those who reside there'.

I was surprised by the tone of this letter. After all, it was only a few months earlier that Alistair and Veronica had been running their restaurant and lettings room business at their house. If that had been a success then surely it would have contributed to increased traffic flow and noise from their customers. Poacher turned gamekeeper, anyone?

The council received Alistair's letter on 25 November, a mere three days before he was murdered, and they wrote to Andy Burnett the same day, notifying him of his neighbour's objections. Burnett received this letter on Saturday, 27 November, just a day before the murder. Now I know a planning dispute over some decking may not be the most serious matter and should not provide a motive for murder, but people have been killed for less.

Hidden among the planning files I found a scrap of paper

with the name and mobile phone number of a detective sergeant written on it. Clearly, and not surprisingly perhaps, the police had found this dispute to be of interest. We needed to speak to Andy Burnett.

That day we made an unannounced visit to the police headquarters. I was told to return the next day, which Tom and I did. I then spoke to a representative from the media department, who did grant us the time to lay out our case for the release of more information, not only about the envelope and the discussion around it, but on other aspects of the crime as well. I left there thinking we'd been listened to, our case was well reasoned, and I thought we might actually be getting somewhere. But I never heard from them again.

We went to the Bank of Scotland offices where Alistair had worked and were told in no uncertain terms that we could not film or speak to anyone. If ever you decide that you want to research and write about unsolved murders then please grow a very thick skin – you'll need it!

Andy Burnett did agree to speak to us, so we headed back to Nairn and The Havelock. Dressed in trainers, combat trousers and a tee shirt, he cut a very self-assured and relaxed figure. He ushered us to the flat above the hotel. This was the accommodation he shared with his wife and two young children; there was another baby on the way. Tom and I were shown into the comfortably appointed lounge, where sofas, soft furnishings and children's toys took up a lot of space. We were told to make ourselves at home while Andy attended to a bit of business.

After a few minutes, he joined us and made himself comfortable to the point of being almost horizontal. He looked as if he had nothing to hide and nothing to be fearful of. On being told that we were filming the interview for a possible TV documentary, he was agreeable and completely unfazed.

Andy told us that he used to be a milkman in Guernsey, but he'd sold his milk rounds and decided to move to the mainland. He and his wife had been looking to buy a business and had explored quite a large part of northern Scotland. They'd researched Nairn on the internet and fell in love with the town on their first visit. They had two dogs and thought a place near the links and the beach would be ideal. It had taken a couple of viewings of The Havelock before they decided to make an offer for what they thought was a fantastic building. Eight weeks later, in early 2004, it was theirs.

I asked how much money he'd paid for The Havelock. 'Lots of money, too much money,' was the answer. Now, in 2009, he and his wife had grown tired of living above their business; they felt like they were never truly off-duty, so The Havelock was back on the market. He told me it was to be his first and last venture as a licensee. I asked if the events over the road had soured his impression of Crescent Road and Nairn, but he was adamant they hadn't. He told us his wife was Canadian, his kids had dual citizenship and that he thought his family's future might lie there.

He explained his version of the events of the evening of 28 November 2004. Apparently, he went to The Shambles every Sunday evening for a drink or two. He enjoyed a bit of peace and quiet away from his own busy bar, albeit he was only about a hundred metres away at the opposite end of Crescent Road. He was imprecise as to the time he got to The Shambles that night, although as he was being joined by friends (a couple and their three children) for a pre-dinner drink and they had a table booked in The Havelock for 7.30 p.m., he thought he would have been walking past Alistair's house not long before events began to unfold at number 10.

No sooner had Andy got to The Shambles before a man left. A minute or two later, this man returned to collect his cigarettes, which he'd forgotten. Andy was precise when he said his friends had joined him four minutes after he had got to The Shambles. In what seemed to be a contradiction, he said he had been in The Shambles for 'Less than the time it took for the barman to pour me a drink,' when someone ran in and said to him, 'You've got to come back, somebody's been shot.'

Andy didn't quite believe this, but he thought he'd better take a look. As he made his way the short distance to The Havelock he could see events unfolding on the Wilsons' front doorstep. He went over and saw that Alistair was clearly in a bad way; he noticed his neck was swollen, he was ashen and convulsing. Andy also noticed blood on Alistair's hand but he could not be sure whether it was from the gunshot wounds, a clot or another type of injury. Two police officers were present and were both on their mobile phones. Alistair's wife Veronica was also on her phone. Two female customers from The Havelock were attending to Alistair. Andy took hold of Veronica by the shoulders and asked what had happened: 'A guy rang the doorbell,' she told him.

Andy reckoned it took about twenty minutes for paramedics to arrive. When Alistair's body slipped from the stretcher, he helped put him back on it. He noticed that the metal clasp on Alistair's watch strap had come undone so he put it back on properly. By this time Alistair was in the ambulance.

At a properly managed crime scene, with police officers in attendance who know what they're doing, rather than being constantly on the phone, none of this almost certainly well-intentioned interference by members of the public would be allowed. With every human touch and interaction the risk of contamination, destruction or removal of vital forensic evidence is massively increased. I appreciate that the first police officers to arrive may not have been used to such a crime, but that is still no excuse for not managing the crime scene and the victim effectively and professionally. Allowing onlookers like Andy Burnett to actually touch the victim is grossly unprofessional. We will probably never know what damage to the investigation was done that night.

Andy was less than complimentary about the standard of the police investigation. This might not be surprising because for a while he was regarded as a man with a potential motive. He faced what he called 'constant interrogation and accusations' from the police. 'Things were getting serious' so he had to get his solicitor involved. He gave many statements to the police and if there was the slightest discrepancy, they would question him again and again. 'Have you got connections?' they would ask. They were obviously going to question Andy, because on the Saturday he had received the letter detailing Alistair's objections to his decking and the next day, his neighbour was shot – 'I just thought you could build whatever you want' had been Andy's rather naive approach to it all.

As The Havelock overlooks 10 Crescent Road, Andy had seen an awful lot of the forensic examination of the scene and claimed the police had recovered shell casings but had missed one because it lay hidden beneath a leaf and was only recovered days later. I have no way of verifying this. He went on to explain that some days after the murder the house was thoroughly cleaned in preparation for the return of Veronica and the children. As part of this process he saw the brass front doorbell being vigorously polished, only for it to be completely removed by forensics officers a couple of days later. He thought that was an entirely pointless exercise as any potential evidence would surely have been removed when it was cleaned.

Andy had pretty forthright views on just about everything. He called into question the veracity of Veronica's account and timings. No less than nine people, all of whom he could name and whose details had been given to the police, had been in Crescent Road at the time of the murder, he maintained. Therefore, he felt it inconceivable that no one had seen the gunman. He was certain that if the gunman had been on Alistair's front doorstep for as long as Veronica claimed, he would have been spotted and also argued that the gunman would have been silhouetted by light coming from Alistair's hallway, whenever the front door was open. All of this went towards him conjuring up a theory that the gunman must have been in Alistair's house, therefore Veronica might have known his identity, although he did accept this was just his theory. He questioned whether Veronica could have seen the gunman disappearing down Crescent Road towards The Shambles, as she had claimed, if she had been upstairs. The gunman would have disappeared by the time she got to the front door and her stricken husband, he felt.

Clearly, by the time I interviewed Andy, he had had nearly

five years to ponder over events repeatedly and work up his own theories. He expressed surprise that Veronica had chosen to stay on at the house, which is still her home today, and wondered whether she would be fearful of the gunman returning: 'Unless she's got balls of steel and doesn't give two hoots.'

There had been some issues between Andy and Veronica since Alistair's murder, which revolved around another planning application. I asked his opinion of Veronica. 'I've no grievance with her,' he replied, 'but I'd like to know a minute-by-minute account.'

Andy summarised the case by saying, 'It doesn't make sense.' He was keen to emphasise, 'You don't get shot for no reason.'

Tom and I had to spend quite a bit of time capturing pretty and panoramic shots of Nairn to go into our short film, which would be pitched to Channel 4. I drove the car while he filmed out of the window. I'd far rather have been getting in front of more witnesses and potential sources of information, but I knew this was a necessary evil. On our last evening, Tom and I ate together before he returned to the bed-and-breakfast to take care of backing up that day's footage and giving the production company a call to let them know how we were getting on.

I decided to spend the evening in the bar previously known as The Shambles. Now, it was called The Bandstand Bar of The Braeval Hotel. The bar is named after the famous Nairn landmark that sits on the grassy links and features in so many images of the town. Tom and I had not been shy that week – we'd let it be known to everybody we came into contact with who we were and what we were doing. It pays to advertise.

As is so often the case, even to this day, people were happy to talk to me about Alistair Wilson's murder. And always, I'm only too happy to hear what they've got to say. Mostly it's gossip, rumours and theories, but I take the time to listen. Occasionally I will be pointed in the direction of a witness who saw or heard something about the crime or someone who knows something about Alistair the man. That night something very different was to happen.

The bar was busy. Groups were gathered at tables and a number of men were propping up the bar at the opposite end to where I was sitting. I had a pint, nattered to people, and then had another pint. The atmosphere was cordial. People were nice and relaxed and I reckoned I'd earned the right to have a drink. This was coming out of my own pocket, mind you, the little bit of expenses we'd been given didn't stretch to alcohol. The barman and I were getting on famously.

As the night wore on, I was contemplating going back to the B&B to get my head down. I visited the bathroom. Many years had passed since my undercover days so I no longer saw danger at every corner. I didn't recce every toilet I ever went into, looking for potential escape routes.

Suddenly a deep Scottish voice boomed out from behind me: 'Don't turn around.' Mid-stream, I had no intention of doing anything of the sort. 'This is all I'm going to tell you. It was an in-house job, but we just couldn't prove it. Wait here for one minute after I've gone.' His footsteps disappeared out of earshot. I finished my business, washed my hands, taking longer than usual, and then counted to thirty. As I walked back into the bar, my mind was churning over what I'd just been told. The tone and forcefulness of this man's voice had left me a little shaken. Perching back on my stool, I ordered another drink: sleep could wait.

I made sure I was the last punter left in the bar – I wanted to confirm what I thought was blatantly obvious, that the man in the bathroom had been a cop. The barman and I each had a wee dram that I paid for. We talked about how busy the bar had been and what a good clientele he'd had in that night. He was in closing-up mode so time was not on my side so I grabbed the bull by the horns and said, 'Do you get any police drinking in here?' 'Oh yes,' he replied, 'one of that group at the end of the bar is a police officer.' I wasn't going to push him any further for a name, I had to respect that this officer clearly hadn't wanted to show his face to me. It's exactly the same principle if somebody calls me anonymously with information: I have to respect their anonymity. Naturally, I wished this officer had approached me openly, that would have been great, but he may have felt he would have risked his job by doing that so now I only had a scrap of a line to feed off. I thanked the barman and took the very short walk back to the B&B. As so often in the past few days, I walked by the front door of Alistair Wilson's house.

So, what could an 'in-house job' mean? Tom and I discussed it over breakfast. You might think the obvious assumption to draw would be 'in-house' as in Alistair's house. I never assume anything for as a wise old detective once told me, way back in the day when I was aiming to get into the CID, 'Assumption is the mother of all fuck-ups.' Besides, any such assumption would infer that Veronica Wilson was not a witness of truth. Again, I make no apologies for referring back to DCI McPhee's statement of 1 November 2005. That was clear and unequivocal: Veronica is not involved in any way. Could it really be the case that McPhee was saying that, yet other police officers were thinking the opposite and were saying so to relative strangers like me? Surely not. You may get sick of me saying this, but I'll reiterate once again: Veronica Wilson is innocent.

Could 'in-house' refer to The Havelock House Hotel? Andy Burnett didn't shoot Alistair, because he was in The Shambles bar at the time. And there's no way he paid somebody else to do it either.

Could 'in-house' refer to Alistair's work at the bank? Now, there was an avenue that needed exploring.

Tom and I made a last-ditch attempt to get an interview with the former DCI Peter McPhee, now plain old Mr McPhee, who had got himself a job working for the local authority in the Emergency Planning Unit. We were unsuccessful, but he did speak to the local media. I suspect the words he uttered then, nearly a decade ago, still ring true today. He said, 'I am convinced that it will only take one phone call to bring the killer to justice.'

Tom and I returned to London full of hope and expectation that we'd get this very low-budget documentary commissioned. Our four days in Nairn had been very productive. We were well positioned to put some new stuff into the public domain. Of course we hadn't solved the case, but we had some interesting threads, in particular the 'in-house' line. We'd also interviewed a person who the police had regarded with some suspicion. Tom put together a taster tape, which was a compilation of the scenes we'd shot, all weaved together into a nice little film, just a few minutes long. This would go in front of the people who were commissioning the First Cut documentaries.

We waited, and we waited, as is so often the case in the world of television. Both of us knew that our work on the case could be seen as a bit controversial and we most certainly had unfinished business to attend to, but we would delve deeper once we had the £50,000 from the channel, with which to make our film. I know £50,000 sounds like an awful lot of money, but for a twenty-four-minute documentary, it is a tiny budget. Tom and I were really up for this, though; we believed in what we were trying to achieve. Questions came back to us from the channel, via the production company. They wanted to know whether or not Veronica Wilson would contribute and we couldn't give them a definitive answer. I sensed some people were feeling a bit uncomfortable with the whole project and I was right. The head of the production company called me with a very apologetic tone to his voice. I knew what was coming. Apparently, the channel's lawyers were somewhat uneasy with what Tom and I proposed to do, so our idea was not to be commissioned.

I was really pissed off. There we were, willing to put ourselves out there, big time, to find out all we possibly could, to potentially unearth all kinds of things in the name of trying to move an unsolved murder investigation forward. But no, they wouldn't back us. I understood that the potential legal issues were considerable, I realised there was always a risk that the police could suddenly arrest someone and our documentary would have to be canned, although I thought an imminent arrest extremely unlikely. However, my disappointment ran deep, very deep, and the experience left a bitter taste.

After five years, the police weren't actively investigating the murder anymore, and now we weren't going to be either. Did anybody care about this crime?

CHAPTER SEVEN

NEEDS MUST

I t was 2010. For a while another former colleague from the cops had been pestering me to go into business with him. He had a small yet highly bespoke company which specialised in gathering intelligence for various businesses, including lawyers, insurance companies and accountants. I'd worked for him on a number of successful cases, including one where we identified and seized many millions of pounds' worth of assets for a liquidator.

I have an awful lot of respect for the majority of former military service personnel that I've met and worked with in the security industry. Sure, I've worked with some grunts who I wouldn't give the time of day to, but in the main, those I've worked alongside have been focused and professional. However, one particular former soldier was soon to be exposed as a complete fraud. He was claiming that he'd been seriously injured fighting for Queen and Country in Iraq, that the army had been negligent and had not succeeded in caring for him properly, had failed to compensate him accordingly and as a result he was firmly on the scrapheap of life. If he was to be believed, then the injuries he had suffered to his back, neck, arms, legs, torso, virtually his whole body, which still caused him considerable pain and therefore rendered him unable to walk or work, were deserving of sympathy and compensation.

This ex-squaddie was suing the MoD for an absolute fortune. His case was based around the argument that the army exposed him to unnecessary risk in the first instance, which led to his injuries, followed by a breach in their duty of care towards him. This was a multi-million-pound claim. It would be the MoD's insurers who would foot the bill, were they found to be negligent, but this in turn would have some effect on the cost of insurance to the MoD and therefore have an impact on the public purse. The former private had gone to a national newspaper and told them his sob story. Hook, line and sinker, the newspaper fell for his tale of woe and published a two-page spread complete with photographs, telling how this national hero had been so shabbily treated.

With the court case looming, the insurers wanted his case looked into as they considered their position. Should they defend the claim, or save themselves the potentially massive costs of a trial and a finding against them and settle out of court? They came to my friend's company and he delegated this task to me. I did some open source searching. Open source intelligence gathering is pretty much what it says on the tin: you search open sources on the internet. But it's a lot more than just a Google search, which almost anyone can do. There's some pretty sophisticated software out there that can direct your searches deep into the recesses of the internet that are not available to the average person using a regular search engine. There are many security companies out there who can steer you in the direction of this software and train you how to use it. It's astonishing and frightening just how much information about us is out there if you know where to look. Of course, the usual social media sites like Facebook and Twitter can be very revealing, depending on how much of your life you share on those, but there's far more personal information that can be found by those who know where to look. And it's all perfectly legal.

Almost immediately I struck gold. I discovered that this poor wounded soldier was, unbelievably, advertising himself as a scuba diving instructor. The trouble was, he was in Bulgaria. So, I hatched a plan. I contacted a colleague of mine who was ex-army, with whom I'd worked on a number of security tasks. We'll call him Glen. He is one of the coolest-headed men I have ever met. Completely unflappable under pressure, hard as nails, he possesses a disarming manner which endears people to him. He's seen more than his fair share of active service in a wide range of conflict zones and is somebody I would always want covering my back. I explained the situation to him and I was delighted to hear that he had a bit of downtime between security contracts. And he was right up for this job: he felt that this damages claimant was potentially trashing the reputation of the military.

Glen was going to work undercover, posing as an ex-army bloke who wanted to learn how to scuba dive and had always wanted to visit Bulgaria. What a nice simple cover story. As

Glen was almost certainly going to be wearing trunks or a wetsuit most of the time, he wouldn't be able to carry any covert cameras or other recording equipment, so somebody else would have to gather the vital corroborating evidence. No problem, a female colleague and I would pose as a holidaying couple, not connected to Glen in any way, and we'd film all the footage we'd need. The plan was all going swimmingly until I put the proposal and the costings to the boss of the company. There wasn't enough money in the pot for me to travel with a female colleague, so I would have to do all the filming on my own.

I was not happy; I did not relish the prospect of posing in Bulgaria as a middle-aged man holidaying on his own. Not only that, I felt Glen needed at least two colleagues to cover his back. But I was fighting a losing battle: it was just me and Glen or the job would go to someone else. Begrudgingly, I agreed. I decided that I'd use my tried-and-tested cover story of being a writer if anybody asked, a writer searching for inspiration for his next story in a nice warm climate. Glen and I booked our flights and hotels separately, of course, but we caught the same plane.

We'd discovered from the internet that the subject of the operation worked at a couple of hotels, one in a coastal resort, the other a bit further inland. Glen arranged to meet him at the inland hotel for some tuition in a pool. He'd done a great job on the target, innocently asking him in general conversation what make of car he drove, what times the target would arrive for a lesson, all the kind of stuff that might make my life a bit easier. I drove to the hotel, spotted the target's car and hurriedly did a recce of the surrounding area.

Opposite the hotel, I found a small park with some trees and a few bushes from where I could keep eyeball on the vehicle. Then I waited.

After about thirty minutes the target came out of the hotel, swinging an oxygen tank in each hand. After opening the back of his car, he slung them into the boot with ease. He made another couple of trips to and fro, loading a pile of kit in his car. This man did not look disabled in any way whatsoever. In fact, he looked a picture of health and I was capturing it all on camera. That was until a very irate elderly man grabbed my shoulder and started ranting at me in a language I did not understand a single word of. He was very, very cross. I was extremely disappointed that I'd been compromised, but I had to get away because this man was creating an almighty scene. How long had he been watching me? Did he have anybody else with him? Who the hell did he think I was? A spy, the secret police or what? He was doing his nut and I was in danger.

I jumped in my hire car and drove as steadily as I could, by which I mean speedily but safely, using all the police training I'd had over the years. All the while I was trying not to bring too much attention to myself – no screeching tyres or handbrake turns. I noticed a blue saloon car with two men inside was following me so I turned this way and that down side roads, trying to see if they were actually following me or whether I was a bit paranoid. Still, they were in my rear-view mirror. Shit! I'm in Bulgaria, I've been seen secretly filming someone and I'm not in the most enlightened or liberal country in the world, I thought. Who are these people behind me? I decided to drive straight back to my hotel. If I made it there, I could take stock, call the office and decide what to do then. That's if I was going to make it that far. I told myself not to drive like a lunatic or do any more anti-surveillance; for the time being, I'd just drive sensibly.

But still, the blue car was there, for what seemed like an eternity. I drove along mile upon mile of open country road. Should I pull over and let them pass? No, thousands of hours of firearms training and basic common sense had taught me that it's harder to hit a moving target so I wasn't stopping for anyone. Besides, what if they stopped behind me, then what?

As I approached the resort where I was staying the traffic began to build up. I was on the main road into town and the traffic was slow. The car following me was no longer on my tail, but two or three cars back. I'd done a recce of the resort when I first arrived and had the rough layout and a sense of direction as to what lay where in my head. I sensed an opportunity. Without indicating, I took a quick left turn, one hundred yards, then another left, then another. Back on the main road, I made myself a bit unpopular by reversing parallel to the kerbside, which forced a few cars to move over a bit. But now I would be in a position to see the blue car if it emerged from the road that I had just come out of. This time I'd be behind them and the followers could become the followed. I waited; no sight of them. There were plenty of other roads they could have taken if they were looking for me and I hoped I'd shrugged them off. The blue car and its occupants did not reappear.

With the adrenaline still pumping through my veins, I somehow drove very sedately back to my hotel. I decided I was going to be extremely cautious about what I did and who I spoke to from here on in.

For the next couple of days Glen would be receiving his diving instruction in a rather nice outdoor pool. I got myself there in plenty of time to bag a poolside sunbed, set up my camera and slap on a bit of sun cream on my middle-age spread and balding head. Along strode our target, oxygen tank in each hand, and stacks of other kit across both shoulders. He put the kit down and dived headlong into the pool. Capturing it all on camera, I filmed two days of this. Towards the end of Glen's course, he had to do an open-water dive from the back of a rigid-inflatable boat (RIB). He was alongside a number of other students that our target had been teaching elsewhere. I was perfectly positioned on the beach overlooking the harbour as the target loaded more than a dozen oxygen tanks and, well, you've got the picture by now. If we needed a final nail in the coffin of his fraudulent claim, it came when the target towed the RIB containing eight people and all their diving kit by hand, using a rope, from one end of the jetty to the other.

At the end of the operation everybody except the fraudster was happy. Glen got a diving qualification and we both got paid. The boss was delighted because his clients – the insurers – were extremely satisfied. Then I received a proposition.

The owner of the company called me in to a meeting in his very discreet offices. He asked if I would be willing to form a subsidiary of his existing company, with us both 50/50 partners in this venture. The company would basically perform the same kind of inquiries as his main firm, but it might afford me the opportunity to earn more money as a partner, rather than a hired hand. In other words, I'd get a share of the profits.

I mulled it over for a while. This venture would require me to get out there into the big bad world of business and drum up customers. I decided to give it a go. Our start-up costs were minimal because my new business partner had the necessary infrastructure in place. So, I gathered together the contact details of everyone I had ever met and set about getting in front of those who I thought might require our services. How I hated it! I mean, I really hated it. I'm fine sitting in front of media executives or publishers and pitching story ideas. I'm also comfortable in front of live TV cameras and giving commentary, insight or opinion, but parading in front of insurers, lawyers, accountants or wealthy individuals, trying to sell investigation or security services is something I'm not any good at. I can feel myself cringing as I write this now because all those uncomfortable memories are coming back to haunt me. After flogging this dead horse for a while I apologised to my partner and we called it a day.

A wonderful friend, who I'd first met way back in the days of *Murphy's Law*, who held a senior position in the BBC, had long been encouraging me to write drama rather than act as a consultant on other people's work. I used him as a conduit to pitch an idea for a play to BBC Radio 4. To my delight, it got commissioned. Now, don't go thinking you'll make a fortune this way because you most definitely won't, but it was a start. *Blue Flu* was my imagining of what would happen if a disillusioned police service (who are forbidden from striking by law) all reported in sick one day as an act of unofficial industrial action. Broadcast in 2012, it was well received. I was asked to write another play for Radio 4 and *The Beat Goes On* was transmitted later that year.

The next level of progression would be writing for TV, a rather better paid thing to do than writing for radio. So, I pitched an idea to the BBC and was commissioned to develop my project as a potential three-part TV series. This was a whole lot better than trying to sell my services to lawyers and accountants, etc. I hadn't forgotten about Alistair Wilson, of course – I was watching from afar.

CHAPTER EIGHT

A DECADE ON

The anniversaries of unsolved murders are often used by the police as opportunities to renew public appeals. People's memories may be jogged and in cases that have been unsolved for many years, the police often hope that allegiances have changed, that previous loyalties that ensured someone kept quiet may no longer exist. It has been known for an ex-wife to come forward with crucial information many years after a crime has been committed, because she no longer lives in fear of a brutal and dominating husband. Members of once fiercely loyal organised crime gangs can fall out with one another and this may encourage a person in the know to finally spill the beans.

Every police service has a media machine that tries its best to stage-manage the release of information as they see fit. Invariably, journalists want to know more than the police will reveal and Alistair Wilson's case was no different, certainly as far as I was concerned. I thought that the tenth anniversary of his killing would be a good opportunity to try and put some pressure on the police to finally reveal all they knew about the mysterious envelope. At this point in time none of the information about the colour, shape and size of the envelope had been released by the police. Nor had they disclosed the details of the conversation between Alistair and Veronica about the envelope. Everyone was in the dark, hence so much gossip. I felt this information could be crucial in trying to piece together who the gunman was – a professional hitman, someone with psychological or mental health issues, a person with a grudge who was on a revenge mission, or whoever – because up until now, most of the media commentary about the gunman had largely been speculation.

So, in November 2014, I started trawling my list of media contacts in Scotland. I reminded them of the upcoming anniversary and made myself available for a quote or two. I'd been widely commentating on crime and policing in the media for fourteen years by then, so I had some credibility and my name was firmly out there.

The police in Scotland had recently undergone major change. All of the country's eight police forces had been amalgamated into one organisation called Police Scotland, who now had charge of the case. I'm a big fan of large centralised police forces – in the future, I think we will see more forces merge. Moves towards that have already begun, I would argue, with some forces pooling resources that deal with major crime and sharing other units with specialist skills. If I had my way, I would merge all of England and Wales's police forces into one organisation. I'd unify every force in England, Scotland, Wales and Northern Ireland. Money could be saved because one enormous force would have incredible purchasing power when it came to uniforms, equipment and services. Standard operating procedures would be applied universally (with a bit of tinkering for rural areas as opposed to inner cities) and personal fiefdoms, which some small forces currently are, would be a thing of the past.

Scotland's eight forces had merged on 1 April 2013. Little old Northern Constabulary had disappeared forever. Officers who had served in Scotland's major cities, who had experience of murder and other serious crimes, were now available to be dispatched the length and breadth of the nation. The Northern Constabulary had called upon other forces in the past to help them with their investigation into Alistair Wilson's murder, most notably Grampian Police, who were asked to carry out a review of the Northern Constabulary's investigation in 2005, but now potentially more experienced detectives could be tasked to solve the murder.

I should add that it has been far from plain sailing for Police Scotland since its inception, so those who would argue against my case for amalgamation and centralisation of forces may have grounds for saying I'm entirely wrong.

The first chief constable of Police Scotland was Stephen House. In July 2015, a couple – Lamara Bell and John Yuill – were travelling along the M9, near Stirling, when their car left the carriageway. A call was made to the police but the information was not passed on as it should have been and consequently, it was some four days before their bodies were discovered. There was outrage. Stephen House resigned some weeks later.

In 2017, four officers, including an assistant chief constable and a superintendent, were suspended amid allegations surrounding the use of the firearms range and missing equipment. Two other officers were placed on restricted duties. There were more as yet unproven allegations made about the police being called to the home of a senior officer. All of this attracted huge publicity north of the border.

Also in 2017, Police Scotland's second chief constable, Phil Gormley, became the subject of a number of investigations after allegations including bullying were made against him. Eventually, he was placed on special leave. He resigned in early 2018 after attracting months of negative headlines.

I wondered whether this fairly new and somewhat embattled organisation would have a more enlightened attitude towards the release of information than the Northern Constabulary had shown. We would soon see.

Police Scotland got their press release out on 24 November 2014, four days before the actual anniversary. Perhaps they were trying to seize the initiative, to be ahead of the game. They rolled out a couple of heavy hitters, two chief superintendents, one of them a detective. Here's their press release; it contains some corporate police speak, but it's interesting in what it reveals. Please stick with it…

> Under the new procedures introduced by Police Scotland, the case is subject to a homicide governance review, which is looking at previous investigation strands to ascertain if all possible lines of inquiry have been thoroughly exhausted.

That is a damning indictment of the Northern Constabulary's investigation if they did not thoroughly investigate all lines of inquiry.

Police Scotland continued:

> Detective Chief Superintendent Gary Flannigan, of the Specialist Crime Division Major Investigation Team, has overseen the strategic review.
>
> Flannigan said: "Ten years on from his death, Alistair's murder remains unsolved. Police Scotland is determined to ensure that every possible avenue has been explored in our continued efforts to find answers for Alistair's family and friends and to bring whoever was involved in his murder to justice."

Flannigan decided to beat the police drum: 'Over the course of a decade, detectives have worked tirelessly using a wide range of methodologies, seeking expert help from throughout the UK and considering advances in forensic science all in an effort to help detect this highly unusual crime.'

He went on: 'We will continue to appeal to anyone who has information to come forward. Despite media appeals throughout the past ten years at times appropriate to our investigative strategy, playing an important part in helping us generate information, no new critical information has emerged at this time.

'While the information coming to us has slowed down, I know that someone somewhere knows exactly how and why Alistair was shot. Unsolved homicides are never closed; they remain open in the hope that the vital piece of evidence surfaces to help bring the investigation to a conclusion.

'Somebody out there knows something or perhaps suspects they know why Alistair was murdered. It's not too late to come forward, and for the sake of Alistair's family I'd appeal to you to pick up the phone.

'All unsolved homicides are subject to review and this case is no different. One of the key aims in the introduction of Police Scotland was to increase access to specialist services and detectives who have a vast array of investigative skills and experience that can be deployed.

'Police Scotland took on responsibility for a number of unsolved and unresolved homicides in April 2013 and it is only right that we subject those cases to scrutiny and review to provide answers for victims' families and bring those responsible to justice.'

Chief Superintendent Julian Innes, Local Police Commander for Highlands and Islands Division, said: 'The murder of Alistair Wilson remains an active and ongoing inquiry. As a result of becoming Police Scotland, the Highlands and Islands Division has had greater access to specialist support and that's being used to progress this investigation.

'We are all committed to bringing Alistair's killer to justice. The support shown by the local community has been there from the start and remains as the impact of this dreadful crime is still felt. I remain hopeful that someone will have the vital piece of information that can make a difference.

'Crimes of this type are rare in the Highlands and Islands as indeed they are across Scotland. We are absolutely committed to working with our community planning partners to keep our communities safe.'

So, what were the police really telling us? Well, the investigation was 'subject to review' and 'open and ongoing'. In practical terms that should mean that a review group is poring over all the evidence previously gathered, looking for any lines of inquiry that they think need following up. The reviewing of homicide investigations is now a routine part of modern-day policing. It is not the job of a review group to solve the crime, but to see if anything has been missed. A seasoned review group investigator told me that lines of inquiry are usually overlooked because of bad practice, genuine mistakes or a lack of experience on behalf of the original investigating team. A full-blown review will look at everything. This will include all the information gathered and stored on the computer system and all the other information, like witness statements, which can be stored in boxes. With a case like this, it is entirely likely there will be 'tons to read'. The review will also examine all the decisions made by the senior investigating officer at the time.

All the intelligence gathered by the original investigation will be rigorously interrogated to ensure every scrap was thoroughly researched and actioned appropriately. This will undoubtedly include all the gossip, rumour and theories put forward at the time and in the ensuing decade.

Crucially, all the exhibits and forensic evidence will be scrutinised. My friendly review officer told me, 'Throughout this process we will be asking ourselves the question, "What can we do today that we couldn't do in 2004?"' In terms of DNA, the answer is quite a lot. In 2004, if an item was seized that had mixed DNA profiles from a number of people on it – say, an item of clothing worn by a victim that had been touched by the assailant, police, paramedics and even other witnesses – then it would have been impossible to separate that mixed evidence out into identifiable, individual profiles. Recent advances in forensic science have now made that sometimes possible. Even in cases where a full DNA profile cannot be obtained (a profile that would be evidentially strong enough to irrefutably prove a person's involvement in a crime), it is now possible for scientists to identify enough characteristics to say to the police that there is a 'strong possibility' that a particular suspect was at the scene because a DNA profile is 'fairly well represented'. This is not evidence but intelligence. In circumstances such as those it would then be the job of the police to gather other evidence in sufficient quantities to support a charge.

In recent years the rules around fingerprint evidence has changed. Previously, sixteen matching characteristics had to be identified between a fingerprint found at a scene or on a weapon and that of a suspect. That rule has now been abandoned and there is no quantitative standard. This means in some cases a mark featuring less characteristics will be accepted by a court. New methods of retrieving fingerprints have also been developed. The science has moved on enormously since my days of being a murder squad detective, when you hoped the scenes of crime officer would find a fingerprint when armed only with a brush and a tub of powder. High-resolution digital cameras, various light sources, filters and complex software can all now be used to discover and enhance fingerprints.

Had the review officer I was talking to been involved in looking at Alistair Wilson's case, he said he would have been very interested in studying any mobile phone data retrieved at the time. At around 7 p.m. on a Sunday night in November, I would imagine the mobile phone traffic in Nairn would be very light compared to some bustling UK city. The task of poring over it in fine detail would therefore be a manageable one. Mobile phone calls are routed through a cell tower, invariably the cell tower closest to where the call is being made from. Police retrieve what is called a 'cell dump' from the mobile phone provider, who operates any given tower. This cell dump is a record of the calls routed through that tower. It can be a laborious process to work through every call, eliminating the perfectly innocent calls, one by one, until such time as you are left with calls made from unidentified or suspicious phones, which would warrant closer examination.

My review officer would have recommended that cell dumps be obtained from cell towers nearest the scene, three hours either side of the crime. If those searches did not identify a suspect phone being used – for example, an unregistered pay-as-you-go phone, then he would have suggested the search fan out to towers covering a wider area, even perhaps so far as Inverness, once again three hours either side of the murder. Past experience caused the review officer to comment, 'As soon as he's shot Alistair, the gunman is on the phone. He makes the call and bins the phone.'

With Alistair Wilson's case now 'under review' and the investigation 'ongoing', it was clear Police Scotland were deploying considerable resources. I was very pleased. If we believe this statement from the police, then in 2014 this was no longer a case that had been put away, only to be reopened when new evidence came to light, as it had been in 2009. By the way, the fact that there was no investigating team in 2009 makes a mockery of DCS Flannigan's claims when he says that detectives worked 'tirelessly' for a decade.

I thought it was interesting that there were two references to essentially the same topic. The police said they were working, 'to ascertain if all possible lines of inquiry have been thoroughly exhausted,' and were checking that 'every possible avenue has been explored'. Was this some kind a tacit admission that they were less than confident in the detective work carried out during the previous ten years? It would be some kind of admission, were that the case, for this is not some long since forgotten crime committed back in the 1970s, taken off a shelf, dusted down and reviewed. This is a modern twenty-first-century case that should have had the best resources and investigative minds applied to it from the start and throughout the ensuing decade.

There was of course no hint of admission that they had in any way failed in their quest to find the killer, nor any apology for failing to charge anyone. At times I despair of the police and their inability to openly accept that sometimes they get things wrong. I know what a challenging job policing can be – there's over fifty years of policing experience in my house alone. But I desperately wish the police would look at themselves in the mirror a bit more often and accept that sometimes they just weren't good enough. It takes a strong person or organisation to willingly admit that sometimes they just weren't as good as they should have been. To me, it seems the police only apologise or make admissions when forced into a corner, consequently any apology they then make looks almost begrudging and disingenuous. Surely the failure to catch Alistair Wilson's killer after ten years, and that's what it was, a monumental failure, was worthy of some recognition? That's how the majority of the public I've spoken to in Nairn see it: a failure, plain and simple. I think they would warm a bit more towards the police if they were a bit more willing to admit that publicly.

Three days later, I was quoted in some of the newspapers, including the *Daily Record* and *The Scotsman*. Among the questions I wanted answers to, which featured in the papers, were: 'What was in the envelope?', 'What was written on it?' I was further quoted in the *Daily Record*: 'I can understand the police withholding that information 10 years ago, but now they should release that information as a matter of course. It must be relevant.' I'd also told journalists that I wanted the details of the conversation between Alistair and Veronica Wilson, but you have to realise that as a contributor, you have no editorial control whatsoever over what a journalist may or may not put in their article. I've always accepted that without complaint. Over the years, one newspaper in particular has attributed a couple of headlines to me using words that I most definitely would not have said, but I usually shrug my shoulders and crack on. In the main I've had a very good relationship with all the media outlets I've ever worked with and I hope that continues. We need each other, but more of that later.

Anyway, the police do take great notice about much that is said and written about them in the media. Cases that are high profile sometimes get more resources allocated to them than less noteworthy crimes. Take the case of Madeleine McCann, for example. Her parents have had a media machine all of their own and I think as a result more police resources have been ploughed into that case than many others. When David Cameron was prime minister he made public pronouncements about the case and suddenly more public cash was thrown at it. In a perfect world, every murder or missing person case would all receive equal funding and attention. The reality is very different.

A few times in the past I have commented about the Madeleine McCann case in the media, but people still ask my opinion to this day. After travelling to the complex where the family stayed in Praia da Luz, I examined the area thoroughly. I have sat in the restaurant at the same table where Gerry and Kate McCann sat that night with their friends in May 2007. I have walked the route they took to and from their apartment to that restaurant many times. The McCanns' three young children were out of the sight and earshot of their parents. I have absolutely no hesitation in saying if identical circumstances had arisen in the UK, then I'm certain the McCanns would have been subject to a police investigation where the offence of neglect of their children would have been considered. Gerry and Kate McCann have, of course, paid a terrible price for their actions that evening. I think the likelihood of Madeleine ever being found alive is remote in the extreme.

A journalist put my request for more information about the envelope to DCS Flannigan. He said, 'I sense that it is something that could be potentially interesting to the public, so we'll look at that. If it doesn't harm the investigation then there would be no reason not to share the limited information that we have.'

I was bitterly disappointed to hear DCS Flannigan describe the information as 'limited'. For years, I had hoped that the whole envelope information could be absolutely crucial. However, this information was not to be forthcoming for a while.

Veronica Wilson, Alistair's parents, Alan and Joan, and his sister Jillian gave a statement to the media as part of the tenth anniversary appeals:

> Despite years of searching for answers, the question which always remains is why? We are confident that someone somewhere knows the identity of Alistair's killer, a man who is still at large. He has killed once. He may kill again and cause another family the heartbreak we have endured.

Let's take a close look at this statement from the family. The police media machines are often very keen to stage-manage what relatives say – they don't want the family going off-message and letting slip anything that may hamper the investigation. I'm convinced in this case that the family press statement will have been pored over by senior detectives and the police media department. Be aware that misinformation is sometimes given out, but those occasions are rarities. Such an example might be if the police were on the brink of an arrest and they didn't want the offender being tipped off, so family and police might come across as if they remain completely baffled.

Now, back to the Wilson family statement. They say the killer is 'still at large'. Do the police definitely know that to be the case? If so, surely they must have a suspect in mind, somebody who is roaming the streets free, as opposed to a suspect currently in prison for some other offence, or one who has died or been killed? That line could be highly relevant. Or am I overthinking this? Were the police in 2014 clueless as to the identity of the killer and consequently, they just let the family say what the family thought? I doubt it.

The family were 100 per cent right when they said in their statement, 'He may kill again'. When researching unsolved murders for my previous book, *On the Run*, I investigated two cases where killers had murdered once, were not caught for those crimes and then went on to kill again. Their names were Christopher Nudds and Levi Bellfield. I cannot think of two more utterly repugnant wastes of space. Dangerous wastes of space at that, for they have killed at least five people between them. Fortunately, they now languish behind bars.

CHAPTER NINE

HUNTED

When you're a self-employed freelancer like me, you have to have lots of fingers in many different pies. The hope is that by spreading your name and what is hopefully a good reputation across many different media outlets, production companies and decision-making executives, people will think of you when they want commentary or opinion, when they're developing a drama or a documentary, or when commissioning radio plays.

This has meant that over the years I have been to countless meetings to discuss very many projects, most of which have never got further than the development stage. But that's the nature of the beast: you won't win the lottery if you don't buy a ticket. It makes life all the sweeter when a project gets the green light and you're hired.

In 2014, I got a phone call from a TV production company called Shine, who explained that they were developing an idea for a show where members of the public would pretend to be fugitives and would go on the run. Shine said they would need a team of former or serving police, military, analysts, intelligence experts and the like to try and track these fugitives down. They asked if I would be willing to meet them and have a chat about it. I was very interested in the idea so I agreed.

A few days later I met the would-be producer and his assistant at their offices in London – both very sweet people, who I liked immensely. We spent a couple of hours chatting away, having a laugh, while also being very serious about the project. They got a camera out and filmed me answering a few questions. We left on the best of terms and they promised me they'd be in touch.

I didn't have to wait long before they were back on the phone, keen to speak to me again. We had another meeting and thereafter things moved along at a fairly rapid pace, which is refreshingly different for TV, where the wheels can often grind very slowly, to many people's frustration. The show got commissioned by Channel 4, we had a practise week and we were ready to go: *Hunted* was about to come alive.

Originally, I was to be one of the ground hunters – the men and women out and about on the streets of Britain, making inquiries, doing all sorts of clever covert stuff and who will hopefully lay their hands on the shoulders of the fugitives, bringing their time on the run to an end. But Production decided they'd rather have me in headquarters as a deputy to the chief. I guess they thought a man of my somewhat advancing years might not be athletically capable of running through streets and fields in pursuit of sometimes much younger fugitives and maybe they had a point. Somewhat reluctantly, I agreed, and the filming of Series One began.

I thought *Hunted* would spark a debate among viewers about the powers of the state and the surveillance society in which we live, which we replicate on the show. But I was wrong. The conversation among viewers was overwhelmingly, 'What would you do?' – in other words, how would you evade capture, which is a far more light-hearted, fun and engaging chat to have. What do I know, eh? That's why I'm not a TV executive.

Hunted proved popular, particularly among the eighteen to thirty-five-year-old demographic, although my ninety-year-old mum loves it too, but she's probably a bit biased. A second series was commissioned. This time a new chief was needed and I was asked if I'd step into the role. I jumped at the chance and was readily promoted. A mate of mine quipped, 'Only in television would you ever get promoted to chief.' But I was very happy because I was keen to bring my personality and leadership style to the fore. I always keep a watching brief over what my team are doing, although I know when to step aside and let the hugely talented individuals do their thing. Though constantly reminding myself not to get in the way, I'm always there to offer advice, formulate strategy and give the benefit of my experience, but leadership is often about standing back and allowing talent to flourish. I'm always there to fight my team's corner, if need be, too.

Anyway, Series Two was filmed and broadcast in 2016. Again, it proved very popular and my public profile began to rise a bit. After filming wrapped, I rolled on to a consultancy for a drama that had been commissioned by Sky. Called *Guerrilla*, it was written by the American writer John Ridley (who won an Oscar for writing the blockbuster movie, *12 Years a Slave*). He was an absolute joy to work with and it was very humbling to spend time alongside such an incredible writing colossus. The fabulous actor Danny Mays appeared in *Guerrilla* (as police officer Cullen) and he and I spent some happy hours together on set. What a brilliant actor he is! He can convey a raft of emotion when standing still and saying nothing.

I'd written another play for BBC Radio 4, which we were due to record as soon as filming on *Guerrilla* had finished, so I plucked up the courage to ask Danny if he would appear in my play. To my absolute delight, he agreed to play the lead role. *Hard Stop* was a courtroom drama where I put an armed cop on trial for murder and Danny was to play him.

Writing for radio is such a wonderful thing to do because you are never constrained by scale, which you might be in film or TV. If I want a helicopter, a burning shopping centre or a convoy of surveillance vehicles, it's all achieved by merely pressing a sound-effect button, rather than spending a lot of money which you'd have to do if you were writing for the screen.

Danny and the rest of the cast were wonderful in my play, as they brought my words to life. They improved my writing no end. It remains a source of great pride that *Hard Stop* featured in Radio 4's 'Pick of the Week' and was described as 'masterful'.

In the summer of 2017, we shot two series of *Hunted*, one being a celebrity version, which was a first. Then, in early 2018, *Celebrity Hunted* was nominated for a BAFTA. It is very satisfying that the work of so many people has received some recognition.

People often ask me if I enjoy *Hunted*. My response is always the same: I look back on each series with exhausted affection. The hours are long and the pressure relentless because we all desperately want to catch those pesky fugitives. Many of the team have day jobs in the fight against crime and they feel that their professional reputations are on the line. The fact that our every move and word is caught on camera just adds another layer of pressure. It is of course a great privilege to be involved in such a ballsy and innovative project, which calls for a brave production company and a courageous broadcaster. Fortunately, millions of viewers thoroughly enjoy the show, so it's a great honour to be part of something that entertains so many. I've no idea how long the *Hunted* juggernaut will roll on, I'll just throw myself into it wholeheartedly for as long as it lasts.

My publisher is fearlessly courageous and the publishing of my memoir on my time undercover in the Met, *The Gangbuster*, all those years ago opened doors for me which I still walk through today. After my second book, *On the Run*, which focused on ten unsolved murders, it was agreed that I could return to this idea for my third, this time focusing on five new unsolved murders. These cases would cover a wide range of victims, male and female, young and old, different methods of killing – stabbed, shot, suffocated – and a wide geographical range. The first case on my list was always going to be Alistair Wilson.

I threw myself into researching the five murders I'd selected. I hadn't been short of subject material because of the continually high amount of murders that go unsolved. I'd kept a file on my previous research into Alistair Wilson's killing, so I refreshed my memory by poring over that. I dug out the contact details of the reliable sources I had forged over the years, telling them I would soon be back in town.

Not only did I have to strike a deal with my publisher, I also had to negotiate with my wife. From past experience I knew this book was to be an expensive venture because there was going to be a lot of travel involved – I had to visit the scenes of the crimes, make all my inquiries and often treat sources to a drink or a bite to eat. With travel to Nairn on the horizon, I knew the cost of flights, car hire and accommodation wouldn't come cheap.

We reached an agreement whereby I would be allowed to spend the first advance payment on my travel and research, but that was all. I was a bit concerned that this wouldn't be enough cash to enable me to travel as often as I'd like, but a deal was a deal and if you've ever met my wife, you'll know she's not the sort of woman to cross. I'd just have to be a bit creative when it came to juggling finances.

If you're ever thinking of writing a book then please, please do, but remember this, an advance is just that, it's an advance of money which is later reclaimed by the publisher from future book sales. You won't receive a penny in royalties until the publisher has been paid back the advance in full. If the book bombs and doesn't sell enough copies for the publisher to reclaim the advance, then it's just tough on the publisher – that's the risk they take. Your book will have to sell an awful lot of copies in order for the advance to be earned out and then, and only then, will you receive a royalty payment from any other sales beyond that. But if you feel compelled to write then you must. Good luck!

It was great to be reaching out to my sources once again with some positive news. This book would be written and would be published, that I could guarantee, which was in stark contrast to my previously unsuccessful attempt to get a TV documentary made. Having been brought up to speed on some of the local Nairn gossip, I made a solemn pledge to be back in town in a couple of weeks. I made it plainly clear how committed I was to unearthing anything I possibly could about Alistair Wilson's murder.

CHAPTER TEN

PROGRESS

Nairn was always going to be the first location I visited for my new book, which at this stage I firmly believed was to feature five cases. My deep affection for the place has never diminished. In fact, it's only grown with each trip I've made there. I made all my rather costly travel arrangements and rang a source to let them know when I'd be arriving. What this source had to say was very interesting indeed.

First, I was sworn to secrecy, in that I could never reveal this source's identity and by this, the source meant never, ever, no matter what the circumstances. So, I gave my word. I reminded the source that, during my days undercover in the force, I had disobeyed a judge who demanded that I reveal a person's identity during a criminal trial and I'd flatly refused. Even when the judge threatened me with prison, I did not back down. My stance in that trial caused the case to collapse and allowed the defendants to walk free. A file was sent by the court to the Director of Public Prosecutions (DPP), who considered whether I should stand trial for contempt of court. For some months I had the cloud of a potential jail term hanging over me until eventually, the DPP ruled that it would not be in the public interest to put a dedicated undercover cop on trial for keeping his mouth shut. My principles hold as firm today as they did back then in my undercover days. When people's lives are at risk, it is of course a no-brainer, I'll never disclose my sources. The same applies when livelihoods and reputations are at stake. If I don't have people's trust, I have nothing.

My Nairn source told me I was free to use the information that I was about to receive however I saw fit. This source then relayed a quote to me: 'Alistair was killed because of the finances of Livingston Football Club. That is common knowledge amongst some members of the legal profession in the Central Belt [the Central Belt runs from east to west across Scotland and incorporates Edinburgh and Glasgow]. The reason nobody has come forward is because they don't want an assassin arriving at their front door. The gunman didn't intend to shoot Alistair, but something went wrong'.

I asked my source if I could have access to the person who had given this information. That was a complete non-starter because it would reveal that my source was relaying the information to me. This information was therefore destined to remain hearsay evidence and one must always exercise extreme caution when dealing with information relayed second or third hand. Regardless, the information was potentially valuable to me, not only in research terms, but in monetary terms as well.

I scoured every inch of the vast amount of media coverage Alistair Wilson's murder had ever received. My search confirmed what I thought when I first heard this information: nothing I had ever read or seen had suggested or reported professional football as a possible motive.

I discovered some links that were potentially very interesting. Pardon my geographical ignorance, but I didn't know where Livingston was. I found out that it was some twenty miles west of Edinburgh. Alistair had worked in specialist lending when he was posted to Edinburgh by the Bank of Scotland. A quick conversation with a friend who works in accountancy and audit confirmed that any lending to a professional football club would definitely be regarded by a bank as specialist lending. And there was more. The Bank of Scotland had forced Livingston FC into administration on 3 February 2004, almost nine months before Alistair's murder.

It was time to head north to Nairn.

Years of experience in the media had taught me the value of publicity. Widespread coverage sometimes encourages people to come forward. I posted on Twitter that I was heading to Scotland to research the case. Almost immediately my phone rang. It was a woman who works in Scottish radio, who I'd previously spoken to about various crimes. She'd seen the tweet and asked me all about my trip. Did I have any new information? Yes. Could I tell her what that information was? No, but I did say I had a possible new motive for the crime. She was very keen to get me on air.

I also spoke to a wise and seasoned journalist from Trinity Mirror newspapers, who are now known as Reach plc. In Scotland, they publish the *Daily Record* and its sister paper, the *Sunday Mail*. I told the journo about the potential new motive and he was keen to do a substantial piece featuring this revelation. Soon afterwards, a *Daily Record* headline screamed, 'Former Cop Close to Cracking One of Scotland's Most Notorious Murders', which wasn't quite how I would describe my position, but the case was getting fresh publicity at least.

There were downsides. Dealing with all the media enquiries left little time to dig deeper into the information, but that could wait. My trip was booked so I had to get on with it. In the cab from my home to the airport I fielded calls from TV, radio and newspapers. Most of the journalists were very persistent in wanting to know what my potentially new motive was, but I wasn't going to tell them; I had to investigate that information and that would take time. Besides, if this turned out to be some golden nugget that could move the case forward significantly, I would probably choose to reveal all in this book and not give it away for free to a journalist from a local newspaper (writing books is now what I do when I'm not tracking down 'fugitives' on *Hunted*, which only takes up a few weeks of the year). Some journalists were particularly unhappy that I wouldn't elaborate on the motive, but I've got a lot of experience in dealing with the press so I stood firm and resolute in the face of some very probing and sometimes trick questions. Journalists have a job to do and I understand that they all want an exclusive, but I had to remain in charge of when and how I released information to them. I put my phone on airplane mode and looked forward to an hour's peace during the flight.

That was all I got. As I waited to get my luggage at Inverness Airport, I switched my phone back into regular mode and the answerphone messages came flooding in. I was beginning to get a little concerned that this five-day trip might be swallowed up entirely with dealing with the media rather than getting in front of witnesses and other sources, but I'd created all this press interest so I shouldn't be complaining.

So, I picked up my hire car and headed to Inverness city centre, where I'd arranged to meet a man who used to work in the Bank of Scotland with Alistair Wilson.

CHAPTER ELEVEN

THE BANK

Alistair Wilson's work for the Bank of Scotland was an obvious potential reason for his murder. In fact, I would have regarded it as the first place to look for a potential motive, had I been a detective on the case. To this day, when I first meet people in Nairn or Inverness and I tell them what I'm doing, their initial response is often, 'Oh, the banker! Yes, I remember that.' For many, the job title has become indivisible from the man.

I can't say I'm a big fan of banks. But who is? There can be very few of us that haven't suffered as a result of the banking crisis of 2008, but that of course was some time after Alistair's murder. What I wanted to know was the culture and working practices of the specialist lending, business banking and other specialist sections of the Bank of Scotland in the time leading up to the killing.

Prior to 2017, I'd been pretty unsuccessful in speaking to

any Bank of Scotland employees. I'd been unceremoniously told to vacate the bank premises back in 2009, when me and Tom Randall paid the Inverness offices a visit. But when I started my social media campaign with a vengeance in 2017, it didn't take long before a former bank employee contacted me. We arranged to have a natter over a coffee on my next trip. I followed his directions to a café.

Angus, as I will call this rather avuncular man, did not speak about his former employer in the most glowing terms. He'd taken a job with the business section of the Bank of Scotland in Inverness following a drink-driving conviction, which had put paid to his previous post, where he drove to meet mortgage and insurance customers. As a result, he'd taken a considerable pay cut, which meant that his new role with the bank was taken out of necessity rather than choice.

He began by describing the offices, which were on the middle floor of a three-storey block: 'There was a lock on the front door. More senior people had a key although I ended up getting a key because I was one of the early starters. The bank liked people to work from 8 a.m. to 6 p.m. so the business clients had greater access to bank staff.' (Angus didn't know if Alistair Wilson had a key.) After accessing the main door, there was a keypad into which employees punched their code: 'It was a large office, which had over a hundred people in it. Everybody was in the business banking section of the bank. We were sat in pods of six people, three either side of the desks. Alistair sat on a pod a few feet away from me. There was a team leader for every four pods.'

Once at his desk, Angus would turn his two screens on and log in, using his name, bank number and password. Password controls were strict: if you did not change your password every twenty-eight days, you would find yourself locked out of the system the following day.

I was particularly interested in what Angus had to say next: 'We covered the whole country, all of the UK.' I wondered if Alistair might have had some dealings with Livingston Football Club while working in Inverness. Clearly, this could not be discounted.

Angus went on to explain that he started in the personal banking section, but had been moved to the business section of the bank once the skills from his previous employment had been recognised. When he arrived in business banking, he had a limit of £5,000 that he could sanction in terms of loans or overdrafts, but he soon realised many of the customers he was dealing with had limits of up to £50,000 on their accounts, so he had his limits increased substantially to £50,000 and could now sanction loans or overdrafts of that size without referral to a supervisor. He said, 'I could lend up to a million quid but it went further up the ladder [for sanctioning]. A business case had to be put for it. Depending on what your grade was, you could authorise overdrafts, convert overdrafts into loans and give business loans.

'Alistair was above me, even though he was younger than me. I think he could authorise overdrafts up to £100,000 without referring it to anybody. If a business had an overdraft and it went pear shaped, there might have been a bit of wrist slapping [from the bank], that's all, but people have no idea [of] the sort of money we're talking about.'

The sums of money that Angus and his colleagues were dealing with on a daily basis were substantial: 'We dealt with the daily banking operations of these companies. Money coming in, cheques going out, and you're making sure everything was hunky-dory. I dealt with oil companies in Aberdeen who were having 30, 40, 50 million pounds going into their accounts on a daily basis.' Rather interestingly, he added, 'You could juggle money around any way you liked, it was numbers on a screen.'

I asked if he'd been personally involved in any questionable behaviour: 'Every bank branch had a series of charging accounts. There'd be an account for unauthorised overdraft fees and an account for returned cheque fees. If a customer was charged £30 for a bounced cheque, that would go into the bank's bounced cheque fees account. Provided you took the money out of that account and returned it to the original [customer] account from where it had come from, you could do that with impunity. It was just a counter transaction and nobody noticed.

'I was working with a company in Manchester and they headhunted me – I'd been stopping some of their cheques. When this company realised I had a Certificate of Mortgage Practice and another mortgage advice qualification, the boss of this firm said he wanted me to work for him. I had an interview and they offered to double what I was earning at the bank. Every single charge they had incurred in the previous year, I refunded. It paid half of my salary.'

Angus clearly saw himself as a bit of a hero to some of the bank customers: 'If somebody had just opened an account and been charged for something, I was like, "Right, it'll be back in your account by the end of the day" – I couldn't be arsed listening to the story, it wasn't my money. I was like Robin Hood, take it from the bank and give it back.'

He was keen to relay another tale of refunded charges, only this time it appeared this tactic was being used to protect the reputation of the bank: 'A company had gone into receivership. My boss said there's no point in getting involved. He said, "Refund all the charges we've taken from them."' Angus then refunded about £4,000 worth of charges, which reduced the company owner's debt from £5,000 or so down to £1,000. He continued: 'The guy still had an overdraft, but it made it look like the loss to the bank was less. As a creditor, the Bank of Scotland were only being shown as owed £1,000 instead of 5 or 6 grand.'

Clearly, there was pressure upon staff to perform: 'We were supposed to watch things like tanning salons. If their turnover changed, it should trigger money laundering systems, but I was so busy, it was non-stop. We had fairly strict rules that we were supposed to adhere to, but nobody really checked on you… It wouldn't have been hard to slide an extra transaction into the payroll of a large company. Just set up a transfer to another bank account, sort code, da de dah de dah! In a really big company, it could easily go unnoticed – you do it all from your keyboard.'

It was all well and good Angus hypothesising about potential wrongdoing, but I wanted to know if he had any more evidence I could rely on: 'I was at my desk, headset on, two screens, working away. An employee was suddenly surrounded by men in suits, had his desk cleared and was hurried away from the building, never to be seen again. I said, "What the hell's going on?" We were told not to talk about it – the bank didn't like prosecuting people. They don't want anybody knowing there's anybody dodgy at the bank. They want people to think everybody's clean.'

He wanted to give me his views on Alistair Wilson's murder, although he admitted it was mere speculation on his part: 'I felt Alistair was living beyond his means. Where's the money coming from? If he was moving out of the bank and he was money laundering for somebody, they could say, "We need him to stay there. He's no use to us working for Highlands and Islands Enterprise, or the BRE [Building Research Establishment] or whatever it was called. He needs to be told, 'Stay put.'"

At the time of his murder, Alistair was working his notice at the bank. Upon leaving he was to take up a role with the Building Research Establishment (BRE). This is how the BRE describe what they do on their website: 'we provide a complete range of advisory, testing, certification, commissioned research and training services covering all aspects of the built environment and associated industries'. In other words, if it's got almost anything to do with anything about the building industry, BRE are across it.

The website has this to say about their Inverness offices and Highlands operation – 'BRE Highlands was set up in November 2004 with the objective of facilitating innovation in the built environment in the country which is undergoing a massive period of re-growth and regeneration. At Beechwood Business Park North complex in Inverness, BRE Highlands is ideally placed to act as a gateway to clients for all the products and services BRE has to offer. It is already delivering services to key areas of importance for the infrastructure of North Scotland'.

Before we departed, I asked Angus his opinion of the Bank of Scotland, based on his experience of working for them. His answer was short and unmistakably clear: 'They were iniquitous, they really were.'

The insight he had given me was welcome and helpful, but not particularly insightful regarding Alistair Wilson. Now I needed to find others who had worked closely with him at the bank – I would have a bit of a wait.

CHAPTER TWELVE

OUT OF CONTROL

I f the refunding of charges by Angus and his colleagues in Inverness was questionable, there can be no doubt whatsoever that there was repugnant behaviour being carried out by other staff at the Bank of Scotland, elsewhere in their operation.

When Alistair Wilson, fresh out of university, joined the Bank of Scotland around 1996, it is safe to say he was joining an organisation that was ambitious. Perhaps he felt his own ambitions could be met within the bank, but it is beyond doubt that during his time as an employee, some in the bank behaved appallingly and set it on a course that would eventually lead to fines being imposed, allegations made that it was 'dangerously out of control' and its reputation being damaged beyond repair.

Around the same time that Alistair joined the bank, a fearless and resolute journalist called Ian Fraser began covering the banking industry in Scotland. Ian has written for numerous newspapers and magazines, established a website and blogged courageously. His highly acclaimed book, *Shredded: Inside RBS, the Bank That Broke Britain*, is a must-read for anyone with an interest in the other major Scottish bank of the time and the impact its failure had on us all. Ian's work on Alistair Wilson's employer, the Bank of Scotland, has been no less exhaustive and thorough. He has kindly assisted me in my research and granted me permission to quote him and his work, where appropriate.

In 1999, with Alistair a relatively new and enthusiastic employee, the Bank of Scotland suffered a major public relations embarrassment after a deal to expand their business in the US was brought to a dramatic halt. The bank had explored the possibility of a deal with a company controlled by the American right-wing businessman, author and high-profile preacher Pat Robertson. The plan had been to set up a telephone banking operation in the US, which was all part of the bank's efforts, 'to remain competitive... [And] seek innovative ways of expanding its market'. The trouble was, when clients of the bank, which included local councils and others, became aware of this potential tie-up, they threatened to take their business away. This was perhaps not surprising because over the years, Mr Robertson had expressed many controversial views, including a take on feminism which had given a clear window into his soul. He described it as a 'socialist anti-family political movement that encourages women to leave their husbands, kill their children, practice witchcraft, destroy capitalism and become lesbians'.

Perhaps the final nail in the coffin of this proposed deal

came when Robertson said publicly, 'In Scotland you can't believe how strong the homosexuals are.' He put proud Scots on notice that they 'could fall right back to the darkness very easily'. Somebody at the Bank of Scotland eventually woke up and Robertson was informed the deal would not happen.

The Guardian reported at the time, 'People within the bank cringe that their employer could have associated itself with so dangerous a character as Robertson'.

But the bank remained unashamedly ambitious. A former senior member of staff who didn't know or work with Alistair Wilson told me that around this time the bank was 'a very aggressive place. They definitely put profit before principles'.

In September 1999, the Bank of Scotland and RBS became engaged in a takeover bid for NatWest. Previously, the Bank of Scotland made an unsuccessful hostile bid for NatWest and now found themselves up against their fellow giant of Scottish banking. And they lost out: RBS walked off with the prize that was NatWest.

Ian Fraser tells me that after this unsuccessful bid, the Bank of Scotland 'entered the doldrums, it was drifting'. Other banks were encircling, the possibility of a takeover loomed large.

Following speculation in the press, on 4 May 2001, the Bank of Scotland and the Halifax announced they were to merge. This merged entity would be referred to in the media and colloquially as 'HBOS', although the Bank of Scotland would retain its identity and name in many forms. For the purposes of consistency, I will endeavour to use the Bank of Scotland title hereafter wherever I can. The joint Bank of Scotland and Halifax venture would have a very short shelf life of only seven years before its collapse, government bail-out and subsequent merger into Lloyds. Here, I will focus only on events up until Alistair Wilson's death, but if you would like to read more then I urge you to visit www.ianfraser.org and read his article and timeline entitled 'The Worst Bank in the World? HBOS's Calamitous Seven Year Life'. When Ian first posted this, he was contacted by the Bank of Scotland, who threatened him with legal action unless he took the timeline down immediately. Ian informed the bank that every word was true and therefore he would not succumb to their threat.

I could write reams and reams about the wrongdoing and very suspect practices conducted by the Bank of Scotland in the time leading up to Alistair Wilson's murder, but I will mainly stick to examples of individual and collective negligence or criminality that I hope will paint a clear picture for you of how parts of the bank that Alistair worked for operated.

In February 2003, the Financial Services Authority (FSA), which was the regulatory body for banking at the time, fined the Bank of Scotland £750,000 for administrative failures in part of its customer savings operation. The FSA said these failings 'put 30,000 customers at risk of losing money and also exposed the Bank of Scotland to increased risks of fraud'.

In December 2003, the FSA said it had identified some serious internal audit issues, including lax anti-money laundering controls. The regulator found unacceptably high levels of non-compliance with record-keeping procedures across the Bank of Scotland's retail, corporate and business divisions and an 'absence of effective systems and controls in respect of its policies and procedures'. Andrew Proctor, the FSA's director of enforcement, said the failures, 'were particularly serious as they undermined the bank's ability to comply with the requirements of orders served by law enforcement agencies under the Proceeds of Crime Act.'

These failures were soon to be punished. On 12 January 2004, the FSA fined HBOS £1.25 million for the sloppy internal auditing and lax anti-money laundering controls that it identified the previous month. The FSA stated, 'the widespread nature of the breaches [which mainly relate to the period 2002–03] meant that the Bank of Scotland was unable adequately to monitor the effectiveness of the customer identification aspect of its anti-money laundering policies and procedures in its corporate and business divisions'. The FSA said the breaches were so serious, it considered whether criminal prosecutions were appropriate.

Ian Fraser is firmly of the belief that because the controls the FSA spoke of were so lax, it is fair to assume that money laundering was going on at the bank and that bank staff could have been complicit in such practices. He told me, 'The bank was left to run out of control. The regulatory culture was so weak, bankers could do what the hell they wanted.'

Meanwhile, in the south of England there was an HBOS employee called Lynden Scourfield. A director and manager in a part of the bank's business operation known as the Impaired Assets Division, he worked alongside another bank employee called Mark Dobson.

Clients of the bank who ran their own businesses would approach Scourfield for loans. Before sanctioning any lending, he would insist the bank's clients engage the services of a firm called Quayside Consultancy Services, which was run by a man called David Mills. Mills and Scourfield ran what was later described in court as an 'utterly corrupt scheme', whereby Mills would charge extortionate fees and sometimes demand that his company had to take control of the bank's clients' businesses, which he would then run for his own benefit. This sometimes meant deliberately running the businesses into the ground.

While Quayside charged their enormous and unjustified fees, Scourfield would lend huge sums of the bank's money to these businesses, which were often struggling and would have no prospect of repaying the money. The bank was eventually to lose the eye-watering sum of around £245 million and maybe more. Clients who had been forced into paying grotesque fees to Mills would lose their businesses, sometimes their homes, their health and their futures. But all the time Scourfield, Mills and some of their cronies were getting rich, *very* rich. There were lavish foreign homes, a £2 million yacht, extravagant holidays, cars with personalised number plates, even orgies involving paid sex workers and Viagra. All of this extravagance was largely funded by the financial suffering of HBOS clients.

The TV personality Noel Edmonds has repeatedly claimed that he suffered enormous financial loss after becoming a client of Mark Dobson. HBOS was later taken over by Lloyds and Edmonds is pursuing legal action against them in an effort to reclaim some £300 million. He claims he was driven to the brink of suicide by the bank's actions.

Thames Valley Police (TVP) launched an investigation into the activities of Scourfield, Mills and their cohorts in 2010. It was to be the most complex investigation of the sort that TVP had ever conducted. Millions of documents were examined,

Forensic teams examine the front doorstep of Alistair and Veronica's home on 29 November 2004, the day after his murder. A police officer then checks a nearby drain (below right) on 30th November. *Photos © Andrew Milligan/PA Archive/PA Images*

Above: Carrying on the search for the murder weapon, police search the nearby beach with metal detectors two days after Alistair's murder. The handgun used to kill him was eventually found ten days later in a drain half a mile away from the murder scene.   © *Andrew Milligan/PA Archive/PA Images*

Below left: The ordinary doorstep that became the scene of Alistair's brutal and seemingly senseless murder.

Below right: I was able to have a look at another Haenel Schmeisser pistol, exactly the same as the murder weapon used. Here I'm holding it alongside a Glock for comparison.

Above: An aerial shot of Nairn illustrates the potential getaway routes the killer could have used to flee from 10 Crescent Road (circled in red).

Below: The corner of Crescent Road and the pub, known as The Havelock, opposite the Wilson's home, looking down towards the nearby North Sea.

There are a few different getaway routes the killer could have used to flee from 10 Crescent Road – here are a couple found to the right and left of the house.

over 150 officers and police staff were involved, and the investigation took some six-and-a-half years to complete.

In 2017, Scourfield, Mills and others stood trial at Southwark Crown Court in London. The trial lasted four months. Judge Beddoe was scathing in his comments as he sentenced the guilty parties. He described Scourfield's 'rapacious greed' and said that he had 'got his tentacles into the businesses of ordinary and honest people and ripped them apart.' He continued, 'I do not know when or how David Mills got his hold on you, but that he did. He is the devil to whom you sold your soul, for sex, for luxury trips with and without your wife – for bling and swag.' Scourfield, who had pleaded guilty, was sentenced to eleven years and three months.

But Judge Beddoe had more to say. He said the corrupt scheme had 'ripped apart those businesses without a thought for the lives and livelihoods of those affected…'

Mills was convicted of conspiracy to corrupt, four counts of fraudulent trading and conspiracy to launder the proceeds of crime. He was sentenced to fifteen years.

Others convicted for various roles in the scheme included seventy-three-year-old Michael Bancroft, who was sent to jail for ten years, the other HBOS employee Mark Dobson who got four-and-a-half years, and John Cartwright, who received three-and-a-half years.

Mills's wife Alison also got three-and-a-half years.

The officer in charge of the investigation, Detective Superintendent Nick John, was swift to publicly thank the jury, the Crown Prosecution Service and the wider prosecution team and his officers and staff. Rather pointedly, there was no mention or thanks for the bank.

The fallout from this affair rumbles on. In January 2018, the Police and Crime Commissioner for Thames Valley Police, Anthony Stansfeld, released a lengthy statement about the crimes, the investigation and the bank's involvement. Please remember that while the bank has been through takeovers and changes of name, at the time Scourfield and his cohorts started their criminal behaviour, he and Dobson were very much Bank of Scotland employees.

Anthony Stansfeld said: 'The fraud was denied by Lloyds Bank for ten years, in spite of it being apparent that senior members of the bank were aware of it at least as far back as 2008. It resulted in a great number of companies being ruined, and the lives and livelihoods of their owners and those that worked with them being destroyed. They were pursued for their personal guarantees and lost their houses and possessions as the bank and its lawyers pursued them for all they owned. Families were split up, marriages ruined, and suicides resulted. Throughout this period, it seems extraordinary that the bank could deny a fraud had taken place.'

He continued: 'The victims had written in to three chairmen of Lloyds, laying out clearly what had happened, but were ignored. It was not until the jury found the defendants guilty in January 2017 that Lloyds would admit to the fraud, a fraud in which the bank itself had lost many hundreds of millions. The admission came many months after their own banker [Scourfield] had pleaded guilty. Throughout the police investigation the bank through its lawyers was less than helpful to the extent of being obstructive. This resulted in the case lasting far longer and costing far more than necessary. It is unlikely that even a small percentage of the money stolen will be recovered, it has been well laundered abroad.'

Lloyds appointed Professor Russel Griggs to deal with compensation claims from victims. Some of those victims are understandably furious. This scandalous affair will not be finally settled for some time yet.

Now I appreciate that Scourfield and his abominable cronies operated a long way from the Scottish Highlands, but this was very much a Bank of Scotland disgrace. It involved two of their employees who dealt with businesses. Alistair Wilson also dealt with businesses. Once again, I felt the need to speak with those who worked closely with Alistair at the bank. For all that I had read and heard about his role within the bank, none had given me the detail I craved. Then I was given a name. I was soon to be on that person's trail...

There's another former HBOS employee I'd like to speak to, one who fell foul of the law sometime after he left the bank. Between about 2001 and 2005, Michael Bolton was employed by HBOS in various senior roles, including head of specialist lending. Alistair Wilson had worked in specialist lending when he was based in Edinburgh. There is no evidence to show Bolton was involved in any illegal activity while working for the bank but he was certainly a well-known figure in the financial world. In 2001, he told moneymarketing.co.uk that his lifetime ambitions were to become a Tory MP, a nightclub owner, a golf professional and wine connoisseur.

Maybe it was his ambition that drove him to leave HBOS, taking some other employees with him, as he aimed to set up an online mortgage lender. He was backed in this venture by some heavy hitters from a private equity firm.

Bolton enjoyed a high profile. Tales abounded about conferences with scantily clad young women and a party where a famous girl band performed amid an atmosphere described as 'not much above the level of a raucous stag do'. The world of high finance, eh?

In 2016, Bolton was due to appear at Exeter Crown Court charged with a £130,000 VAT swindle. He chose not to turn up, so was tried in his absence. The court heard how he had failed to pay VAT on some £900,000 of income generated from banking and mortgage strategy services. Bolton had told investigators before he jumped bail that he had paid the VAT money to a Swiss accountant who went by the name of Paulo Greener. There was no evidence to suggest that this person ever existed. He was found guilty and sentenced to two years' imprisonment, but remains a wanted man. He is married to a Brazilian and it is thought that he may have fled there, or possibly to Spain.

If you do happen to bump into him on your holidays, please inform me or the authorities. I'd like to ask him about his time as the head of specialist lending. I wonder if he had anything to do with lending money to Livingston Football Club. The name Paulo is not that far removed from Paul, the name on the envelope. Of course this may be a completely unrelated similarity of no consequence whatsoever, however, I'd still like to get in front of Mr Bolton when his fugitive days are brought to an end.

The prosecutor of the case, Mr Ian Fenney, issued some depressingly familiar words about Bolton's fraud: 'The money has clearly been dissipated and we cannot see any creative method of retrieving it.'

CHAPTER THIRTEEN

QUESTIONS, QUESTIONS...

Once my conversation with Angus the former Bank of Scotland employee was over, I headed to my bed-and-breakfast accommodation in Nairn, all the while fielding calls from the media. It didn't take me long to familiarise myself with the town once again. I unpacked my bag and headed to the scene of the crime. Veronica Wilson's home has become one of the most photographed houses in Scotland over the years, and it's not only the press who photograph her front door – people who have had a drink or two have been known to rush up the steps to the door and capture a photograph as they strike a foolish pose. I'm sure this ghoulish and unnecessary behaviour has been a source of pain for Veronica over the years.

Back in 2005, Alistair's family had been hugely irritated by the artist Damien Hirst, he of preserved shark and pickled cows' fame, when he announced that he planned to use a photograph of forensic officers on the doorstep of 10 Crescent Road as the inspiration for a painting. Alistair's father, Alan, the police and Fergus Ewing, a member of the Scottish Parliament, were joined in their outrage at the prospect of this piece of art. Hirst later announced that he had ditched the idea.

The police were well aware of my trip. They'd asked me to email them the questions and requests that I wanted to ask of the investigating team. And I'd done that. I'd asked questions that I thought would make this book a more informed tome for you. I felt there was no justifiable reason for them not to answer them all. Here are the questions sent to the police on 2 October 2017. They are quite exhaustive and the questions vary from the matter-of-fact to those that are more personal in nature, but I wanted to cover all the possibilities and I make no apology for that.

I would very much like to interview Veronica Wilson. I have spent a lot of time over the years with the families and friends of murder victims. Many are fully supportive of my work. Please inform Veronica that I would like to speak to her and please furnish her with my contact details.

I would also like to interview Alistair's parents, Alan and Joan. Could they also be informed of my desire to speak to them and be furnished with my contact details. Thank you.

On what date did Alistair hand in his notice to the Bank of Scotland? How long was his notice period?

Had Alistair ever been subject to any discipline procedures whilst working at the Bank of Scotland?

What was Alistair's official job title at the Bank of Scotland?

What was Alistair's salary and benefits package at the Bank of Scotland at the time of his death?

What was Alistair's salary and benefits package going to be at the BRE?

Did Alistair and Veronica have a mortgage or any other loan secured on 10 Crescent Road, Nairn? If so, how much was outstanding on the loan or mortgage? What were the monthly repayments? Who was the lender? When was any such loan or mortgage taken out?

Did Alistair and Veronica put a deposit down on 10 Crescent Road when they purchased it? If so, how much was that deposit?

How long did Alistair, Veronica and Iain MacDonald run the Lothian House business at 10 Crescent Road? Did this business close owing any debts to any person, other businesses or Government body?

Were Alistair's employers at the Bank of Scotland fully aware of his business interest at Lothian House? Did Alistair have to report this business interest to his employers at the bank? If so, had Alistair fully complied with this demand?

The envelope that was apparently handed to Alistair by the gunman has been variously described as blue, green and turquoise. Please confirm the colour and size.

Was anything written or printed on the outside of the envelope. If so, what?

What was the exact content of the conversation that took place between Alistair and Veronica after Alistair had taken possession of the envelope?

Was the envelope opened at any time by either Alistair or Veronica? If so, what were the contents? Could Alistair or Veronica tell what the contents of the envelope were without opening it? If so, what were those contents believed to be?

Did Alistair, his colleagues or his bosses during any of his postings at the Bank of Scotland ever have dealings with the finances of the following professional football clubs: Rangers, Hearts, Aberdeen, Livingston, Dundee United or Dunfermline? If so, please supply whatever details you can.

Is there any current reward on offer for information relating to Alistair's murder? If so, what is the amount being offered and what are the conditions placed upon the payment of such a reward?

Were any DNA profiles recovered from the scene or nearby that remain unidentified? If so, upon what items were these profiles discovered?

Are any exhibits to be resubmitted for forensic examination in the near future? If so, what exhibits?

Is it true that a partial DNA profile was recovered from the murder weapon discovered in Seabank Road? If true, when was this partial profile last subjected to any forensic examination? Are there any plans for this profile to be subjected to any renewed examination? If so, what body will be carrying out this examination and when?

How many rounds were fired in total from this weapon at the scene in Crescent Road? How many rounds hit Alistair? Where and in what order did the rounds hit Alistair?

May I be made privy to the post-mortem report?

May I be made privy to a transcript of the inquest hearing into Alistair's death?

From approximately what distance were the rounds fired at Alistair?

What hand was the gunman believed to have used when firing the weapon at Alistair?

Was any evidence or credible intelligence ever obtained to suggest that Alistair was having an extramarital affair before his death?

When I posed these questions in October 2017, the police had had nearly thirteen years to catch Alistair Wilson's killer. Had they answered my questions, it might have allowed information to enter the public domain which I thought might encourage somebody who was sitting on vital information to come forward. That person might be empowered by thinking that the police were closer to a culprit than previously realised.

The police knew the dates of my arrival and departure. I was trying my best to be cooperative and did not at this stage intend to be anything other than an ally. They rang me. A meeting was hastily arranged for 9 a.m. the following morning at Nairn police station. I juggled the timings of a couple of media interviews because I had to prioritise this meeting. After press photographers had finished photographing me that evening in the darkening gloom, I did what I always do with the hours that remained that night: I had a drink and a bite to eat in the local hostelries. I put my face around town; I handed out flyers to anyone who would take one.

I have a pathological hatred of lateness – I would rather be thirty minutes early than thirty seconds late. This probably stems from my days as a detective when heavy fines would be levied by the boss on anybody who couldn't get to a briefing on time. So, I was early for the meeting with the police. I stood outside the nick having a cigarette as I waited for the minutes to pass. When I saw a respectably dressed man and woman walking towards the front door, I hazarded a guess that they were the officers I was there to meet. I tailgated them and they obviously recognised me. While they arranged an interview room, I waited in reception.

Neil Grieve and Diane Smith were both extremely polite, cordial and they displayed an air of professionalism that was nothing less than I would expect from cops dealing with the most serious of crimes. Diane took copious notes of our conversation. They were not, however, senior detectives in terms of rank and they appeared to defer any potential decisions to their bosses, who clearly had decided not to meet me. It was what it was; I had to deal with whatever officers were put in front of me. We got along just fine.

They reaffirmed that Veronica Wilson did not want to speak to me, and had a message for me: Veronica demanded that I did not name her boys in this book, which I have of course complied with. Previously, the boys have been named widely in newspapers and other media, but a deal is a deal. I can fully understand if she wants to protect them as much as she can. I was also told that Alistair's parents, Alan and Joan, did not wish to speak to me and that I was not to approach them. Again, I was disappointed but respected their wishes.

We discussed the questions that I had previously sent via email. I wanted to know if I was going to get any answers. Neil and Diane informed me that any decision about possible answers would be made by the Crown Office, which is part of Scotland's prosecution system, in conjunction with the senior investigating officer and his deputy. As far as I was concerned, this meeting was not going swimmingly.

I felt I had to make a decision regarding the Livingston Football Club information. My potential new motive line had been all over the media and I knew that the police were keen to hear what I had to say. I made it perfectly clear that I would never disclose my source, no matter what the circumstances. They appeared to pay close attention as I emphasised that point with all the polite and unmistakable firmness I could muster. And then I told them: I had heard that the finances of Livingston Football Club were connected to Alistair Wilson's murder. Their reactions didn't give anything away. Neil and Diane might make good poker players, I thought they were very professional. The ball was now in their court. While I would continue to do my research, they could apply their resources to this, if indeed it was new information for them. They might have already investigated this line of inquiry. Hopefully, time would tell. I made it perfectly clear that I hoped the police and I could work together.

As I left Nairn police station I felt as if I'd just journeyed down a one-way street. Later events were to confirm that my thinking was spot on.

CHAPTER FOURTEEN

LOOSE LIPS

I hurried to a meeting with a film crew from the BBC – lovely people they were too. Initially, I'd been led to believe that I was merely going to give a short interview to be broadcast on the news, but it was to be much more than that. There's a current affairs programme that goes out on BBC2 in Scotland called *Timeline*; it's a bit like *The One Show* on BBC1. This piece was to be scripted, with me walking and talking to camera.

This was more fantastic publicity, which always bears fruit. Whenever a piece goes out in any media format, people get in touch with me. Every flyer I hand out or shove through a letter box has my contact details on it and my social media profiles. These flyers have appeared in the media so I'm really easy to find. My teenage kids think I'm bonkers for having my mobile phone and email address out there for all to see, but I have to be readily contactable because people do give me information. Sometimes I'm given the names of people that others believe have carried out murders – that's why I do what I do.

There can be a downside. People who are frustrated with the criminal justice system or the police often get in touch to ask me to pursue the case of their dead child, missing relative or other similar cases. I simply cannot take each case on – there are not enough hours in the day or cash in the bank. Therefore, with a heavy heart, I often have to explain this and apologise. But I will continue to be as easily contactable as I am, because somebody reading this book may be the person with the key to unlock this or any other case.

The rest of the day was taken up with more media interviews, often with local or regional newspapers. One vastly experienced journalist asked me, 'What would you say to people who think you're just profiteering on the back of other people's misery?' 'Go fuck themselves!' was my instantaneous response. I realised almost as I was saying this that it wasn't a very professional way to respond and that I could come across rather badly if that quote were to make it to print. But I was livid. I didn't fall out with this journo, far from it, we've met since and had a good time together, but that question just hit a very raw nerve indeed as I have only ever been interested in finding justice for victims and their families.

I'm a coffee fiend; I drink it by the gallon. Nicotine and caffeine are not the healthiest stimulants obviously, but they work for me. I was to get through a fair few cups of coffee during my conversations with a very interesting man the following day.

It started with an email soon after the 'potential new

motive' article had appeared in the *Daily Record*. A chartered surveyor who I will call Stuart dropped me a line. Although some people, including Veronica Wilson, will readily identify who this man is, he asked that I change his name in these pages. I am only too happy to oblige. We arranged to meet in The Braeval Hotel.

Stuart explained how the bankers, surveyors and lawyers of the Inverness business community all tend to know one another. They often work alongside each other and they socialise together too. This is hardly surprising. In Scotland it is a surveyor who values a property for sale, unlike most of the UK, where an estate agent suggests a sale price. The bankers can often provide the finance for a purchase and of course the lawyers carry out the conveyancing. They are all inextricably linked. Stuart reinforced this when he said, 'Surveyors, bankers, lawyers, anyone involved in commercial funding, we're all in the same group.' He emphasised that bankers and lawyers, 'Always looked after each other.'

This circle of business associates would often attend rather lavish dinners together, sometimes dressed in their kilts. It was through this closely linked world that Stuart got to know Alistair Wilson. I wanted to find out as much as I could from Stuart about who exactly Alistair was.

At one point not only did Stuart and Alistair occupy the same business world, but they lived only two streets apart. Stuart told me that Alistair was not a central mover and shaker in this business world, in fact he described him as 'peripheral'. He went on to describe one of the bankers' dinners he'd been invited to: 'It was at the Newton Hotel, I was dressed up in my kilty stuff. Alistair said, "You're at my table." I was introducing lots of Bank of Scotland clients to Alistair because he didn't know them – I thought that was a wee bit strange.'

He went on to describe how 'a lot of the bank guys were very much part of the Inverness community, but Alistair wasn't,' but repeatedly stressed how Alistair was 'a really nice lad.' Stuart recalls clearly that Alistair had an issue with one of his ears. He thought Alistair had some kind of hearing loss because in company he would always turn his head in order to compensate for this, so that he could hear conversations clearly.

Stuart said that Alistair tended to look after bank clients rather than instruct survey work, hence he didn't have any direct business dealings with him. He went on to explain that Alistair was omnipresent at functions but always a bit reserved or withdrawn, in stark contrast to the many gregarious characters who occupied this world.

On a Friday night after work many of these men would meet in a pub called The Phoenix in Inverness, but Alistair was never a part of that crowd – 'He never fitted into that.' I was surprised by Stuart's next line: 'Alistair didn't talk about his family, he said nothing about Veronica and the boys.' He continued: 'The Inverness business community is small, everybody knows everybody. It's really tight-knit. We all knew each other so well, except for Alistair.'

Stuart didn't know anything about Alistair's previous work for the bank in Fort William and Edinburgh. But he did know that Alistair was a Glasgow Rangers fan and that 'put my back up' (said more in jest than malice). He continued, 'Alistair was clean-cut, really smart, and epitomised what you'd expect of a bank manager. I never heard him swearing or anything like that. I can imagine him being destined for greatness within the bank. He was a really nice guy, quite young for that position.' He agreed that Alistair's rather withdrawn manner might be overcome as he morphed into his banking role.

Stuart told me that a few weeks before his murder, Alistair was guest of a firm of surveyors on a golf trip to the world-renowned course at Gleneagles. This highly prestigious course and hotel has hosted many a professional tournament over the years, including the Ryder Cup in 2014.

Alistair and his three playing partners arrived at a par-five hole – for the non-golfers, that means you should get the ball into the hole in five shots. It would probably take a group of four golfers about ten to fifteen minutes for them all to complete the hole. Alistair did not play this hole but spent the entire time that it took his playing partners to complete the hole on the phone, on one clearly very important call. Of course, this was antisocial and also broke every golfing etiquette rule you can imagine. That call must have been extremely important. Something clearly very important was occupying Alistair's mind.

His playing partners thereafter named that par five 'Alistair's hole', a name they still use today. The fact that he had been so preoccupied by this call was apparently reported to the police some time after his murder.

Stuart had owned a house of a similar size to that of Alistair and Veronica and offered his views on the Wilson family home: 'The bills on that house would be horrendous. It's always gonna get dry rot. There's no wee jobs on a big house. A big house of that age means a lot of cash.' He explained how the heating costs would be 'considerable', and thought the Wilsons were either 'brave or foolish' to take on a property of that size, especially without a background in food and beverage. On Alistair's income, he opined, 'His basic pay wasn't huge.' Stuart told me that a lot of people from 'down south' come to places like Nairn to escape the rat race. They find themselves a commercial property and start a business, but a lot of these businesses would then fail. He would often discover that these people, 'had had a great idea, but hadn't really thought it through properly'.

A few days before the murder, Stuart received a phone call from Alistair – 'I presumed the call would be about getting a valuation done on his house.' He knew that Alistair was keen to get the house on the market: 'I was loath to take the call because the survey would be a freebie and it was a big house. You'd never charge a banker because if you did, they'd never give you the next survey.'

Stuart went on: 'It [the survey] was on the cards. He'd been asking me for months to do this. I'd resisted a wee bit. I knew I had to do it, they were gonna sell it. It's a big old property. It had traded commercially and failed. I could understand them selling it, downscaling or getting something more akin to a home.' His advice to Alistair and Veronica was that they had missed the marketing point for getting the house on the market and that they should wait until the spring of 2005 before trying to sell. Stuart told me that Alistair's demeanour during this call was 'matter of fact'. The survey 'just had to be done'. They discussed football and there was no hint of what was to come a few days later.

Stuart was, however, in for a surprise: 'I was totally shocked when Alistair told me he was leaving the bank. Jeez! BRE, they had created a role for Alistair and were opening in Inverness.'

Stuart described this change of career path as 'strange'. He went on: 'Building research, that was a shock. Alistair didn't explain why.'

Could the fact that BRE set up their Highlands operation in November 2004 be relevant in some way? It looked like Alistair was to be involved from the outset of this operation. Was he simply given an offer he couldn't refuse, or had life at the bank become intolerable for some reason? Was it a combination of both, or was some other reason behind his decision to leave the bank? I wrote to the BRE, asking for an interview. Sorry if I sound like a stuck record, but you can guess the rest…

Stuart told me that on the Thursday night before he died, Alistair was attending one of those oh-so-familiar functions we've heard about. The event was to celebrate a significant anniversary of a firm of surveyors. A woman was there who was an acquaintance of both Alistair and Stuart (Stuart described her as 'a lovely girl'). She worked for a firm of estate agents. Alistair apparently ended up back at this woman's home after the event. Stuart said: 'It was fairly innocent as I'm led to believe, according to her anyway. Her house was kind of on the way for Alistair and nothing apparently happened. She got questioned [by the police] about why he was there, who's your boyfriend? She didn't have a boyfriend at the time, she had a hell of a time over it.'

The night of the murder there was a fire in Nairn at about 7.15 p.m., which the local brigade attended. Stuart was a volunteer firefighter at the time so he got scrambled. Some firefighters apparently drove their cars rather erratically in their haste to get to the fire station. After putting the fire out, Stuart returned to the station and was sent home. He and his firefighter colleagues were all quizzed by police as to their movements. This was part of the police's search of CCTV in order to account for people's movements. He was highly amused by the fact that some people were caught in places where they shouldn't have been by this CCTV trawl.

Stuart offered up an interesting observation on Alistair: 'I can't remember ever seeing the guy smile. How bizarre is that? Even when I saw footage of him with the kids, he looked the most unhappy guy in the world.' Maybe things were playing heavily on Alistair's mind in the time leading up to his death. The business venture known as Lothian House had failed, he was looking to put the house on the market and it appeared he was disillusioned with life at the bank. Stuart offered this for me to ponder on: 'You never appreciate the trauma folk are going through regarding finance.'

Sometime after the murder, Stuart attended Veronica's house to fit some smoke alarms in his role as a volunteer firefighter. He described part of the interior, including the staircase, which had Georgian glass protection 'all the way up'. With his expertise as a surveyor coming to the fore, he felt the glassware would have provided some sort of sound protection and if something was happening in the hall or immediately outside 10 Crescent Road, then 'you wouldn't necessarily have heard it upstairs'.

Other people who should have known better also had a view on the crime and they weren't afraid to say so, after a drink or two. Stuart explained that in the 2000s he would go away on golfing holidays with cops that he knew. These officers were from the drugs squad, the CID in Inverness and 'all the rest of it' – 'When we'd go away, we would have a few beers and tongues would start wagging.' He said these officers would tell him, 'We just can't prove it. It was definitely her, 100 per cent. We're sure it was something to do with Veronica.' Not only were these officers wrong as the statement from DCI McPhee on 1 November 2005 clearly points out, they also displayed a shocking lack of integrity and professionalism. For officers involved in a murder inquiry to be talking like that to members of the public is potentially breaching the Official Secrets Act and is therefore wrongdoing of the highest order. Stuart offered up an interesting take on all of this: 'This has probably hindered it [the murder investigation] to an extent that it was "Let's prove it's her" and they just can't.'

As Stuart and I bade each other farewell, he had left me lots to ponder.

CHAPTER FIFTEEN

A GUN IN MY HAND

My trip to Nairn was reaping rewards. An enormous amount of publicity had been generated and people were coming forward. Any spare time I had would be spent leafletting and I met a woman in a shop who was keen to speak, but reluctant to give me her name. She told me how her daughter had contacted the police soon after the murder because she had seen a car in the vicinity of Crescent Road, which she regarded as suspicious. Apparently, detectives had been to interview her just days earlier and she'd given a statement. The police had been fairly tight-lipped, but told the woman's daughter there had been a 'significant development' and that they were also travelling to the Black Isle to visit another witness. The Black Isle isn't actually an island, but a peninsula about twenty miles from Nairn. The wildlife is plentiful, and there are castles, museums, a cathedral and towns with wonderful names like Rosemarkie, Munlochy and

Culbokie. It is well worth a visit. Delighted at this news – it was fantastic that the police were being proactive at the same time as me – I rang one of my journalist contacts to give him an update.

After a spot of lunch, I returned to my bed-and-breakfast accommodation. It was Saturday afternoon and I was lying on the bed, highlighting notes, writing some lines on my iPad and analysing what I'd found out in the last few days. To be frank, I was exhausted – I'd had very long days and nights tracking down and interviewing witnesses, speaking to sources, and when time allowed, shoving hundreds of leaflets through letter boxes. I was due to fly home the following afternoon, so I was contemplating how to spend my last night in town. Should I go to my usual haunts, have a bit of dinner and a drink and see who I could strike up conversation with, or was there anybody in particular that I needed to speak to? I'd been using Facebook and Twitter a lot recently in order to make people aware of my trips to Scotland, the fact that I was writing the book and promoting the fact that I'd happily engage with anyone who wanted to talk. Hooray for social media I say, because dozens of people had contacted me this way.

Unfortunately, Nairn County Football Club weren't playing at home that day. Had they been, I would have used the opportunity to hand out some flyers to spectators and catch a game. I'm the chairman of a very large cricket club, whose top team plays at a semi-professional level – an equivalent sort of level to which Nairn County play their football, so I know what it takes to run a club like that. I would have liked the opportunity to swap ideas and experiences and maybe learn what they do well at their club, while hoping to engage with some people interested in Alistair Wilson's murder: that would have to wait.

Suddenly a tweet popped up from a complete stranger, asking me if I was still in Nairn. I said I was and an exchange of messages then followed. This contact was a woman who told me she was the PA of a man who wanted to meet me; he was free this evening and was very interested in the case. It was eventually agreed that I would meet the woman and her boss in a large local hotel which I knew well. It was the Newton, where Alistair and Stuart had attended functions. I'd visited the Newton that week to ask the staff if anybody knew Alistair. The hospitality industry often has a high turnover of staff and the Newton Hotel was no different: nobody working there in 2017 had worked there in 2004.

With a couple of hours to fill before meeting these two strangers, I dragged myself to my feet and set about leafletting the area of Nairn known as Fishertown. This area was only a couple of hundred metres from Alistair Wilson's home and got its name in days gone by when fishing boats would unload their catch for processing in the harbour. The fishing industry has long since disappeared and the harbour is now filled mainly with pleasure boats. There had been some speculation soon after the murder that the gunman might have made his escape by boat, but I never fancied this theory. It all sounded a little bit too James Bond for me, although the police had searched the beaches. You'll recall that a local had categorically ruled this escape route out because of the low tide at the time of the murder.

I had asked my new contact whether her boss would like

our discussions to take place over a coffee or a drink and she suggested a drink. It was nearly time to meet them so I caught a taxi from Fishertown to the Newton. I could have walked, had I not got talking to a local man about all manner of things connected to Alistair's murder, which had swallowed up the time.

I'm a real ale drinker and I've the waistline to prove it. I was disappointed though not overly surprised to see the bar didn't have any so I plumped for a pint of Guinness and weaved my way through the throngs of American tourists.

I'm a fool, I'm a smoker. I started puffing on blotting paper when I was about ten years old and I've smoked just about every inhalable substance known to man during the ensuing years. For a couple of years, I gave up, but the evil habit drew me back. I would like to kill it before the habit kills me. Trouble is, I bloody well enjoy smoking! Pint in hand, I went outside for a fag.

A taxi pulled up and a man and a woman got out. The man was carrying a rucksack that looked pretty full. I hurriedly stubbed my cigarette out. The man and woman walked towards me and we all instantly knew we had found who we were looking for. Warm greetings, handshakes and introductions followed.

I led the way into the hotel and battled through the crowds up to the bar to buy them both a drink. We could barely hear ourselves think because of the din being created by our American cousins. The man, who I shall refer to as Sam, took his drink and strode purposefully out of the bar. He found a vacant meeting room, which he immediately commandeered. I thought we might get slung out by hotel staff at any minute, but Sam was clearly an assertive type and he made himself at home.

Sam had taken a keen interest in Alistair Wilson's murder from day one and his PA had a very good understanding of the case, so we all threw ourselves into theorising and analysing what we knew.

Sam also had a keen interest and a lot of expertise around guns. I had been an authorised firearms officer when I was in the cops, so we had yet more common ground. Sam was very surprised that Alistair's killer had used the Haenel Schmeisser pistol. He laid out his reasons why: 'These types of gun are notoriously inaccurate, they can only really be effective at very close range and because of their low calibre, they cannot be guaranteed to do the job effectively. There are many, many other types of more powerful and effective weapons out there.'

I completely agree with him.

Sam's favoured weapon for carrying out a doorstep killing would be a revolver, a modern version of the type of handgun you see in the old cowboy movies, because unlike the pistol that killed Alistair Wilson, revolvers do not eject spent bullet casings out of the weapon automatically, they retain them in the revolving chamber until they are manually removed. This of course got us on to the subject of the spent cases from the gun that killed Alistair. Whatever happened to them?

Andy Burnett had been pretty certain that the police had recovered shell casings. However, I've pored over press photographs taken the day after the shooting, when forensic examiners in their overalls were doing their thing. I can see no sign of the little numbered and often yellow coloured markers put down to indicate the locations of spent shell casings and other small pieces of evidence that may be found at a crime scene. I've seen some photographs where the forensic guys are looking intently at the grass area to the right of Alistair's front door. The pistol that was used to kill Alistair ejects spent shell casings to the right, as do many other similar guns, so it would make sense that the forensic examiners paid particular attention to that area.

Of course, when these brass casings hit a hard surface, such as the concrete path that leads to Alistair's front door, they can bounce around and jag off randomly. They are highly unlikely to fall into a neat pile in one small space. No media reports or eyewitness accounts ever mention spent shell casings. I've asked the cops about shell casings, but we know all about their refusal to answer questions.

It has been widely reported that Alistair was shot three times. Some reports say twice in the head and once in the body, others the reverse: two in the body and one in the head. As you know, I've also asked the police for sight of the post-mortem report. Not only would it clarify this point, but potentially provide other clues that I'll deal with in a moment. So, three shots equate to three spent casings. Let's just work on the theory that the casings were not found. That can mean only one thing as far as I'm concerned, and let's not forget the envelope was not recovered either.

Therefore, this gunman, after conversing with Veronica once, Alistair twice, and then firing three shots, which caused Alistair to collapse, has had the wherewithal to take with him not only the envelope but three shell casings, which may have fallen haphazardly to the ground. That is no mean feat; it must have required a very cool and calculating mindset.

The gunman may have placed a hand over the ejection point of the gun and caught the casings before they fell. This is not an easy thing to do. If he was right-handed and fired the gun with his right hand, it is really awkward to cross your left hand over and get it into a position to catch the casings. If you are going to catch the casings, it is a lot easier to fire the gun with your left hand and catch the casings with your right. But how many people can do that?

Andy Burnett may have been right in thinking casings were recovered, albeit he claims one was only found under a leaf sometime later. If those casings were recovered at the scene, if they were forensically examined and revealed nothing, then the gunman must have taken considerable care when handling them to ensure not a trace of forensic evidence was left upon them.

Unfortunately, we don't know for sure if Alistair suffered any injuries other than the gunshot wounds. Andy Burnett spoke of blood on Alistair's hand, which could have been from the gunshot wounds, a clot or even a separate injury. It would be very helpful to know if this was an injury that may indicate if Alistair had tried to wrestle the gun away from his assailant. Did he have time to appreciate the danger he faced and tried to do something about it, or was the killer so in control, so ruthlessly efficient and professional, he knew exactly what he was doing? A struggle and a more chaotic set of circumstances may steer us towards thinking this was a sick and troubled mind, rather than an organised crime professional.

The forensic examiners retrieved whatever samples they could from the scene, then the police mounted a sizeable programme of taking DNA samples from local people. The press were requested to respect people's privacy and stay away from the police station in town, where people were attending to be swabbed. A lone cigarette butt was retrieved from near the crime scene in Crescent Road. This attracted a lot of publicity, and the police later disclosed they had obtained an unidentified DNA profile from it. I don't get too enthused about this. Did the gunman calmly draw on a cigarette and then foolishly discard the charred butt before ringing on the front door? He'd taken enough of a risk of being spotted by spending so much time on the front doorstep during the conversations and envelope scenario. I very much doubt he'd had a pre-murder fag.

Sam mentioned more than once that he would use a revolver to assassinate someone. He reiterated the fact that it wouldn't leave any shell casings: 'No brass,' he said. 'You can't leave brass.' All this he said with some relish and what I thought might have been a hint of experience so I looked him in the eye and asked whether he had ever shot anyone. At this he smiled, but offered no verbal reply. His next line took me by surprise: 'Do you want to hold a Haenel Schmeisser pistol, one exactly the same as the murder weapon?' You bet I did. I'd seen police photographs of the gun, but we'd repeatedly been told these weapons were rarely found in the UK and now I had this relative stranger offering me the opportunity to handle one. Sam delved into his rucksack and produced a firearms certificate – 'It's all above board, I'll bring some other weapons so you can compare them.' 'When?' I asked, 'because I'm going home tomorrow afternoon.'

We arranged to meet near the airport the following morning. The next day, Sam drove me to an empty house many miles away in a remote Highland town. He's a man of many talents, one of which is photography, and he set one of the rooms up as an impromptu studio. He then produced the guns. The Haenel Schmeisser slipped easily into the palm of my hand; it was the smallest firearm I'd ever held. The trigger action was light, it didn't take much force to pull it back. The overall mechanical action of the weapon was smooth, the magazine easy to insert and eject. The safety catch was easy to operate too. We were in a house, not a firing range, so we didn't fire any live rounds.

The most attractive feature of this gun to any would-be killer is surely the ability to conceal it. It slipped into my front jeans pocket with ease. I could move around, sit, stand and bend without any hindrance from the gun whatsoever – you would never have noticed it in my jeans, no matter how close you stood to me. It was the perfect weapon to carry around without it ever being noticed. Despite all of this, Sam's preference remained a revolver, because of its superior firepower and the fact that he kept on repeating, which was of course, 'No brass.'

I'm that old that I used revolvers when I was in the cops. Small, two-inch barrelled Smith & Wesson guns that couldn't be spotted by the public or suspects when I was wearing plain clothes. We were taught that when in close range in a dynamic situation without the opportunity to take aim, you must rely on your sense of direction and that you would fire shots in rapid pairs. We were also instructed to aim for an area that encompassed the chest, because that was where the vital organs are and if you hit them, you are most likely to stop a gunman doing what he's doing. Shooting two bullets was also far more likely to stop a gunman in his tracks because the second bullet does not double the impact on the person shot, but multiplies the impact of the bullets by a factor of eight, thereby wreaking havoc on the body of the person shot.

Did Alistair Wilson's killer know this and deliberately shoot a pair into his chest, thereby indicating he had some sort of training or experience in firearms? Or was he an untrained and unstable chancer who shot Alistair as many times as he saw fit, or until the victim collapsed? Please do not get frustrated because I cannot give you those answers now. My investigations and this book were always going to be a work in progress, but I'm confident we will get the answers one day.

But the surprises that Sam could offer were not over: 'Would you like to fly over the scene?' he asked. I didn't really know what to say, but the word 'yes' reluctantly tumbled out. For me, flying is a necessary chore to be endured in order to get somewhere, rather than an experience to savour and enjoy. There's a part of me that remains convinced any flight I take will be my last – a completely irrational way of thinking, of course.

A couple of hours later, we were in a tiny four-seater light aircraft encircling Nairn, with Sam at the controls. To be honest, I was crapping myself. Sam was a relative stranger and there he was, with my life in his hands as we swooped to get an aerial perspective of Crescent Road, Seabank Road (where the gun was found) and the rest of Nairn. It was very interesting to get an aerial perspective but to be honest, I couldn't wait for the plane to get back on the ground!

Later that day, I flew home in what I would regard as a

proper aeroplane, full of hope and optimism. Hope because of the number of people who were engaging with me. I was optimistic because I was learning more about the background of Alistair Wilson and other aspects of the crime.

The following day, I arranged a meeting with my publisher. At this meeting I made an impassioned plea for writing this book solely on Alistair Wilson's case, rather than covering five cases, which was the original plan. My publisher bravely and kindly agreed.

My trip to Nairn had thrown up more questions that I wanted to ask the police, so I asked them to consider these alongside the previous list I'd submitted:

- Did Alistair Wilson's employers, the Bank of Scotland, allow the police full and unfettered access to all information and records relating to his employment, and all matters and transactions that Alistair was a part of, or knew about? In other words, was the bank open and fully transparent with the police? If not, how would you describe any cooperation between the bank and the officers investigating Alistair's murder? (That question stemmed from my meeting with Angus, who had painted a picture for me of a business banking department without stringent checks, procedures and supervision.)

- Did Veronica Wilson ever compile an e-fit [Electronic Facial Identification Technique] or similar image of the gunman? Has any such image ever been subject to an ageing process in order to make it potentially up-to-date? Would the police now consider making any such image available to me and/or the public? If not, why not?

- Were any spent shell casings recovered from the scene? If so, how many and what was the result of their forensic examination?
- When Veronica first opened the front door to the baseball-cap wearing man, did she see the envelope? What were the exact words used during that first conversation? For example, did the man ask for 'Alistair 'or 'Alistair Wilson'?
- Can you please confirm whether there was also an eighteen-month-old child, who was not a child of the Wilsons', present at number 10 Crescent Road at the time of the shooting.

After the standard chasing up, I got a reply:

> Thanks for sending these through. As it's still an ongoing inquiry, we are not in a position to provide answers, but can confirm that the bank have, and continue to support, our ongoing investigation.
>
> We appreciate your cooperation and will investigate any new information you wish to share.

That response left me in no doubt: the police weren't ever going to answer my questions so frankly, I was on my own.

I would plough on regardless.

CHAPTER SIXTEEN

NOVICE, DILETTANTE, JOURNEYMAN OR MASTER?

Many people had offered up their own thoughts and theories to me about the gunman. I'd heard second- or third-hand what the police had apparently said about him and that appeared to be that they didn't regard the gunman as a professional. There were so many contradictions. If I'd been contracted to kill Alistair Wilson then I wouldn't have gone through all the envelope rigmarole, I'd have simply shot him when he first came to the front door.

If Veronica Wilson had been in the slightest bit involved in the planning of this hit, which of course she wasn't, then she wouldn't have answered the front door. When the doorbell rang, she would have simply sent her husband to his death. That way, she wouldn't have seen the gunman and therefore she wouldn't have been subjected to all the inevitable questioning about his description and movements and the trial by gossip and rumour that she's had to endure all these years.

For me, the envelope aspect of this killing is probably the most puzzling. Why would a killer run the risk of leaving what could be a potential treasure trove of evidence behind? If Alistair had taken Veronica's advice and not returned to the front door, for one he might still be alive today and second, the Wilsons could have kept the envelope. The killer must have been pretty cool-headed to be able to take the envelope from Alistair when he reappeared at the front door with it in his hand. Did Alistair hand it back to the gunman before he was shot, or did the gunman seize it after he'd fired the fatal three rounds?

Whatever happened, we know for certain that the envelope was never recovered at the scene. If it had been then maybe the killer would have been caught by now for the potential evidence on that envelope might have been considerable. There could have been the fingerprints or DNA of the killer on it. Had the killer been meticulous about not leaving any forensic evidence on it, maybe the prints or DNA of the person who manufactured, packaged or sold the envelope could have been found. Any person involved in those processes might have been traced and might have created an evidence trail that could be followed to the point where the person who bought it could be identified. There might even have been CCTV from a shop.

It wasn't until 2017 that the police confirmed the name 'Paul' was on the envelope. If the name was handwritten that may have been a giveaway as to the identity of whoever wrote on it. Forensic handwriting analysts can compare the handwriting on an exhibit to samples of a suspect's handwriting and conclude whether or not they were written by the same person. We all have individual characteristics about our handwriting that even when we try to disguise them can leave tell-tale signs. The police did not reveal in 2017 whether the name was handwritten, typed or otherwise printed. This might all have been very helpful to the public back in the early days of the investigation in ascertaining the identity of the gunman. If a particularly distinctive style of handwriting or an unusual type font had been used, a member of the public may have identified that and notified the police. The police have only said the name 'Paul' was on it; I want to know more – the public deserve to know more. This fragment of evidence could be key.

Yet because the killer had the wherewithal to retrieve the envelope and disappear with it, in all likelihood none of the other potential forensic evidence will ever be found. A part of me hopes that the killer has retained this envelope as some form of macabre trophy and when he is eventually caught, it will be secreted away in a bedroom.

We can live in hope, can't we?

I needed some expert opinion about this gunman, assassin, executioner, oddball… call him what you will.

David Wilson is Emeritus Professor of Criminology and Director of the Centre for Applied Criminology at Birmingham City University. He is undoubtedly one of the world's leading experts in his field. You may well have seen him on TV in any number of hugely successful and award-winning programmes. He has written widely in the press and in academic papers about serial killers and lethal violence in organised crime and hitmen. He has advised the police during live investigations and trained senior investigating officers, who then go on to lead murder inquiries. Needless to say, he possesses a towering intellect, yet I've always been hugely impressed when I've watched, listened to or read his work, by the way he conveys information in an easily digestible way. He's also a proud Scotsman and has taken a keen interest in Alistair Wilson's murder over the years.

In 2014, Professor Wilson was co-author of an academic paper entitled 'The British Hitman: 1974–2013'. During their study of this phenomenon, he and his colleagues drew up a list of twenty-seven cases of contract killings, which were carried out by a total of thirty-six hitmen (some killers had accomplices). Some of the data they analysed included the age of the killer and the target, the method of killing, the date, time and place of the hit, what was known about the possible motive and how the killer was caught. They also used whatever data was available about how much the hit had cost. The authors admitted that they were overwhelmingly using data from cases where the killers had been caught and accepted that those who remained at large, like the killers of Alistair Wilson and Jill Dando (the famous TV presenter, who was shot on her front doorstep in 1999), might paint a different profile from the killers they described within their academic paper. This was, however, to be the most exhaustive research ever conducted into hitmen in the UK, so I have no reservations in using it as a credible source.

The average age of the hitmen was thirty-eight. This falls very much in line with Veronica Wilson's estimated age of her husband's killer. The average age of the victims was thirty-six, not very far away from Alistair's thirty years. The average cost of a hit was £15,180, not very far away from the cost that I used to quote for a contract killing when working undercover. To hire me would generally have cost you £20,000, although in all likelihood, you would have ended up in prison for conspiracy to murder.

The vast majority of hits studied by Professor Wilson and his team were carried out with a gun. Discovering a motive was a trickier thing to do although when killers had spoken about this, the majority of cases appeared to be the result of a business dispute of some description. The authors were surprised to discover just how many hitmen who had been caught were carrying out their first such killing and that many of these crimes took place within suburban neighbourhoods as opposed to crime-ridden, deprived inner cities.

A lot of Professor Wilson and his colleagues' research seemed hugely relevant to Alistair Wilson's murder.

Another interesting fact was that the hitman often lived in the same locality as the victim and this was often a reason why they were caught.

Professor Wilson and Co. went on to describe four different types of hitman. There had apparently been much discussion over these, but they finally settled on:

- Novice
- Dilettante
- Journeyman
- Master.

With the copyright owners' permission I've reproduced a table below, which details the characteristics of the different types of hits that were studied.

	NOVICE	**DILETTANTE**	**JOURNEYMAN**	**MASTER**
Method	Shooting	Varied; Shooting/ stabbing/ strangulation/ beating	Shooting	Shooting
Crime scene	Organised/ Some forensic evidence	Disorganised	Organised/ Some forensic evidence	Highly organised/ little or no forensic evidence
Typical target	Varied	Domestic	Business	Varied
Contractor motive	Personal/ business	Personal/ business	Organised criminal activity	Organised criminal activity
How caught	Local intelligence	Varied; Confession/ forensic evidence/ intelligence	Local intelligence geographically stable	Unapprehended/ geographically mobile
Occupation	Unemployed/ casual work/petty crime	Varied	Ex-military/ Occupations involving firearms /crime	Ex-military/ crime

As Professor Wilson and his co-authors were swift to admit, it is difficult to verify some characteristics of 'Masters' because they remain free. It is therefore 'impossible to build up any concrete picture of them as individuals, as opposed to the picture of the type of hits they might execute. However, it would appear one of the major reasons that they evade justice is that these "Masters" travel into the community where the hit is to take place and then leave that community shortly afterwards'.

That would seem to rule out the possibility the killer was a local man, although I reserve the right to keep an open mind on that one. Certainly, the shooting of Alistair Wilson and the dearth of forensic evidence at the scene or on the gun might wholly support the gunman being placed in the 'Master' category. Ex-military or involved in crime, do you know someone who now sounds strikingly familiar?

The authors of this paper were at pains to remind readers that it was an 'exploratory article' and that 'Further research is clearly needed'. I respect their caution, but in Professor Wilson I trust.

Then came Nate...

CHAPTER SEVENTEEN

A VIEW FROM AN ARMCHAIR

I think there's a bit of an armchair detective in most of us – that's probably why cop shows are so popular on TV. I've worked on a few whodunnits, where we've challenged the audience to try and work out who's responsible for a fictional murder or other serious crime.

In November 2017, I was at home wading through the information that I'd accumulated on Alistair Wilson's murder. My phone started going berserk: it was journalists who were asking me if I'd received a 'dossier' from an unknown source, who was apparently calling himself Nate. I hadn't, and I was a bit miffed. This dossier had been sent to a couple of newspapers, the *Daily Mail* and *The Scotsman*; also to Professor David Wilson. I was beginning to feel a bit left out! Professor Wilson would soon discuss the contents of this dossier with John Beattie on BBC Radio Scotland. The police had scrambled to the Scottish offices of a national newspaper, so keen were they to get their hands on Nate's writings.

John Beattie is a former Scottish international rugby player, who now presents a daily radio programme on the BBC. I've often listened to his show, particularly when I'm in Scotland. Mr Beattie is an extremely talented, engaging and very likeable presenter, who has taken a keen interest in Alistair Wilson's murder over the years.

In November 2016, somebody had called his show with information about the killing. The BBC passed this information on to the police, who vowed to investigate 'thoroughly'. This information wasn't broadcast to the public. I can reveal that the caller said Alistair Wilson was killed over deals with a housebuilder. The caller alleged that a former Ulster Defence Association hitman carried out the killing. This hitman apparently was friendly with a farmer, who had been swindled out of a large sum of money due to him for plots of land being sold for redevelopment. The land had been sold at a knockdown price, which had created bad feeling.

That's as much as I was told by one of my confidential sources. I think there's gaping holes in this information and besides, if this 'deal' was connected to Alistair Wilson's work at the bank, then I would like to think it would have been identified by the police early on in the inquiry. In any event, the police had had this information for over a year by the time I received it, which should have given them ample time to investigate. A lack of time and resources on my part meant that I was not going to follow it up; I had to prioritise.

I listened to Professor Wilson's contribution to the John Beattie show. Soon afterwards, he wrote an article for *The*

Herald newspaper. By then I was in possession of Nate's dossier. He had sent it to me but he'd addressed it to my publisher so there had been a couple of days' delay before it reached my home address.

In the A4 envelope Nate had sent there was a covering letter, in which he gave permission for me to use any of the contents as I saw fit. He admitted his work was 'an armchair study', but his dossier ran to eight pages of neatly typed A4 and a concluding page entitled 'Note to editors'. A lot of time and effort had been ploughed into this work. He occasionally interspersed some dry wit into his writing. These were the words of a bright and thoughtful person.

Like many others before him, Nate was trying to 'deduce a credible motive hitherto missing from the case'. There was more than a hint of the conspiracy theorist about some of his opinions as he quickly commented, 'Police have no intention of prosecuting this case'. I read on with an air of caution.

While still on his covering letter, Nate struck upon a quote that I had seen earlier during my research, which had fascinated me. He repeated a line from an article in *Scotland on Sunday* in October 2005, which I thought was so important that I was very surprised it had not been picked up on by any other media outlet at the time, nor since. The *Scotland on Sunday* piece quoted from the Grampian Police report into their review of the Northern Constabulary's investigation into the murder. The Grampian Police review found that the investigation was afflicted by 'confusion and lack of leadership in the first hours'.

Now that's a damning indictment on any police investigation, let alone a murder inquiry. Any homicide detective will tell you how crucial those early hours of a murder investigation can be. I discussed Alistair Wilson's murder and this criticism with a former senior detective who retired after thirty years of service, much of those years on homicide, who has spent the last seventeen years of his life reviewing unsolved or otherwise unresolved cases – 'The first twenty-four hours of any murder inquiry are absolutely crucial, you only get one chance to get it right.'

Because I hadn't seen this 'confusion and lack of leadership' line anywhere other than *Scotland on Sunday*, I tracked down the journalist who'd written the article. He'd moved out of journalism and was now living in the Middle East. Eventually, we spoke. I asked if he'd actually seen the Grampian Police report; he hadn't. How then did he get this explosive line? 'A person who worked in PR at the Northern Constabulary leaked that line to me. He allowed me to use it in return for saying that the rest of the investigation was all good.' I asked if there was any particular officer who had been singled out for this criticism: 'He [the police PR person] wouldn't put a finger on an individual.'

I hope that paints a clear picture for you of how the Northern Constabulary and one of their favoured journalists operated back in the day. I'll let you draw your own conclusions.

I wondered whether there was any other criticism of the Northern Constabulary's investigation in that Grampian Police report, which hadn't been leaked. One of the many people who have helped me with my research submitted a Freedom of Information Act application to Police Scotland, asking for sight of the Grampian report. Bearing in mind this report was now over twelve years old, I thought we might get sight of it, even if it was heavily redacted. Police Scotland refused to let us see even one word of that report. But I'm a firm believer that the truth will out. It has taken very determined campaigners almost thirty years to get to the truth of what happened at the Hillsborough football stadium in 1989 when ninety-six people died and over 700 were injured. They are still fighting for truth and accountability, but ultimately, will succeed, despite police cover-ups and collusion. This Grampian report will one day surface, as will so much more about this crime and the investigations. That is my belief, that is my motivation.

Nate and I are kindred spirits in some regards. We are clearly both fascinated by this crime. He raised a number of points that I have discussed elsewhere, but I'm thankful to him for sometimes sparking a line of thought that I might not have considered or that I may have overlooked.

Nate says, 'Assassins are not in the business of sparing witnesses.' John Childs is one contract killer who adds weight to this argument. In 1975, Childs lured George Brett to a meeting in a factory. Unfortunately, Brett had brought his ten-year-old son Terry with him. Childs shot Brett senior dead and then assassinated his son because he had witnessed his father's murder. Alistair Wilson's killer, however, was clearly willing to spare his wife's life. Killing Veronica after he had shot Alistair would have involved going into the house, searching for her and probably shooting her. An incredibly high-risk thing to do with possibly only three bullets left in his gun. Perhaps he thought their fleeting encounter at the front door would never provide sufficient evidence to accurately identify him. In that regard he has so far been proved right.

Nate raised the question of accent, of which we've heard nothing from Veronica or the police. This indicates to me that there was nothing that stood out in the few words the killer spoke and could potentially indicate a local Scottish accent. To the experienced ear, regional Scottish accents do differ. For example, a Glasgow accent is distinct from a Highlands accent. If the gunman uttered only two words, 'Alistair Wilson', then maybe Veronica was unable to definitively identify an accent. However, in the absence of any information from her or the police, I suggest his accent was probably a local one.

There is plenty of research to show that an envelope has been used in the past to distract a would-be assassination victim. Sam and his PA role-played this in front of me the night we were in the hotel. Try it for yourselves. There can be little doubt that one's eyes are naturally drawn towards an object when it is handed to you, but Alistair Wilson was not shot the moment he was given the envelope, as you might expect an assassin to do, so the distraction element of the envelope is not one I'm convinced by. I sometimes wonder whether the gunman was plucking up the courage to kill Alistair, even when speaking to him, handing over the envelope and going through the subsequent toing and froing. Myself and many others have always tried to make sense of this and the numerous other aspects of this crime and perhaps we're guilty of overthinking it all. If the gunman possessed a disturbed and cluttered mind, then maybe none of this has to make any sense at all.

Nate majored on a development from 2007, which he described as 'dramatic'. It stemmed from a report in the *Mail on Sunday*, which alleged that prior to his death, Alistair Wilson had made contact with criminals in the West of Scotland 'after failing to secure legitimate funding for a business venture'. Nate appeared to be aghast that the police had not put anybody forward to comment on this allegation because detectives had been 'unavailable'. He was also mystified that there had been no follow-up comment on this allegation.

Mistaken identity was a possibility discussed widely in the media in the early days following the murder. I often view such speculation in the press with an air of cynicism, especially in a case such as Alistair Wilson's. When I was pretending to be a contract killer, I certainly garnered enough information from the person 'hiring' me to ensure that I would 'kill' the right person. I would be certain of the target's correct name, address, vehicle(s), associates, workplace and other movements. Cases of mistaken identity are rarities.

That said, Alistair Wilson is not a rare name, especially north of the border. There was another Alistair Wilson who lived only a few hundred yards away from Crescent Road. This Alistair Wilson was apparently an inoffensive man, who for a long time lived with, and cared for, his mother. I've spoken to relatives of his who could not think of any reason why anybody would want to slaughter him. He sadly suffered from alcoholism, which tragically cut his life short in 2017. I've heard stories of the alcoholic Alistair Wilson being refused a drink in bars because he was already drunk, but nothing more offensive than that. In the extremely unlikely event that this Alistair Wilson had done something offensive at which somebody had taken great offence, he would have been easy to find and consequently kill. He looked nothing like the murdered Alistair Wilson, his home circumstances were the polar opposite and I completely discount the theory that the murdered Alistair Wilson was mistaken for his namesake.

I was contacted by a former journalist, who told me that not long after the murder he was doing some research and had discovered an 'Alistair Wilson' among an online chat group. He remembered that this particular 'Alistair' was apparently discussing how to defraud banks. Needless to say, this piqued my interest so I got in touch with a friend who specialises in open source investigations. She soon found a chat group thread with somebody calling themselves Alistair Wilson (this could of course have been a pseudonym), who in 2001 started a conversation with, 'I am not a hacker but I need an experienced one!' This person then went on to ask how easy it would be to spoof IP (Internet Protocol) addresses and how challenging would it be to crack files produced by accounting programs. The email address was not a UK one.

Clearly, whoever started this thread was not the sharpest tool in the box. The former journo told me that he'd printed off the online discussions and passed them on to the murder inquiry team not long after their discovery. The detectives later told him that all the information had been checked out thoroughly. In return for highlighting this information to the cops, they apparently gave the journalist a couple of scoops. He did not elaborate on what those were. How times have changed!

Veronica Wilson was to raise the issue of mistaken identity again soon, but for now, Nate summed up what he thought of this being a likely scenario in one word: 'Impossible'.

Nate wrote to me another three times. He has informed and entertained me and his first dossier helped spark some media interest, all of which I thank him for. I'm convinced he's going to read this book. Doubtless, he will have an opinion or two and so I'm going to pay him the compliment of reproducing here what he describes as 'the only scenario that pulls everything together in a credible way'.

Mr Wilson got into financial difficulties around the time of buying a very expensive property that also doubled as a home business; a failing hotel-restaurant venture that was haemorrhaging cash. He required more funds and these could only be accessed through unofficial channels after being denied these funds from conventional sources. He had previously acquired contacts in the criminal underworld through his job dealing with city businessmen, not all of whom were scrupulous operators. A deal was struck. Mr Wilson would receive a substantial loan (the reported figure was £50,000) in exchange for certain off-the-books 'banking services', possibly money laundering. Mr Wilson was a qualified accountant as well as being a fairly senior bank employee. If anyone knew how to move money around without attracting attention, it would be someone like him. Moreover, this all happened over 10 years ago, when banks were so unregulated they were almost operating as autonomous fiefdoms. At some point Mr Wilson decided he'd had enough of banking and planned to leave the industry. His lenders weren't pleased. Having an 'inside' man in such a profession was highly desirable, not to mention lucrative, and they consequently tried to dissuade him from relocating. Threats were issued to Mr Wilson. He ignored them and paid the ultimate penalty.

Nate always signs his letters off, 'Yours in Pursuit of Truth and Justice'.

We have much in common.

CHAPTER EIGHTEEN

INSIDE THE MIND OF A KILLER

I work with some astonishingly talented people on Channel 4's *Hunted*. The ground hunters are all vastly experienced, tenacious and very determined. Many of my HQ staff are at the top of their chosen field of expertise, be it intelligence gathering, analysis, cyber and more. Even the youngest members of staff who are starting out on their careers have degrees, Masters degrees and doctorates, which all dwarf the handful of O-levels that I somehow managed to cobble together before leaving school at sixteen.

One member of my HQ staff is the remarkably clever psychologist Dr Donna Youngs. Her insight into the personalities and traits of the fugitives is always spot on and contributes hugely to the strategies we deploy in order to try and catch them. It is frightening just how accurate her assessment of personalities can be.

I called Donna and asked if she would be kind enough

to contribute to this book. Her response was far better than I could ever have wished for. Donna works with Professor David Canter, a world-renowned psychologist who has been a major force in the development of Investigative Psychology, which has shaped the thinking of police and the courts when it comes to examining the actions of criminals, offender profiling and geographical offender profiling. Professor Canter has written numerous books, including *Criminal Shadows* and *Mapping Murder*. In the course of his work he has also studied what are so often called contract killings and those responsible. A man very much in demand, he lectures around the world. When Professor Canter speaks, people listen.

While I was well aware of some of Professor Canter's many achievements and Dr Donna Youngs' undoubted skills, I wasn't entirely sure exactly what investigative psychology was, so I asked Donna to write me a definition. Here it is:

Investigative Psychology is the scientific discipline concerned with the application of psychological concepts and theories to all aspects of criminal and civil investigations across the full gamut of crime types, from arson and burglary to stalking, sexual assault and serial murder. It informs the investigative processes, such as interviewing and police decision making, the assessment of police information such as the detection of deception or false allegations and the drawing of 'profiling' inferences about the likely characteristics of a perpetrator from the psychological patterns of actions seen in an offence.

Donna told me that she and Professor Canter would soon be in London and that they had a window of opportunity when we could all meet. It would only be a couple of hours but I was absolutely thrilled. I booked a table at a restaurant convenient for us all and a couple of days later, excitedly made my way there.

Neither Donna nor Professor Canter had studied Alistair Wilson's murder in depth, but they had read some media reports and had a reasonable grasp of events. Where there were gaps, I filled them in as best I could, making sure that I stuck to the facts as they had been reported or as I had discovered. I didn't offer up my opinions very often because I wanted Donna and the Professor to give their views untainted. Our meeting was shortly before the thirteenth anniversary of Alistair's murder so we were not in possession of the additional information that the police would soon make public regarding the envelope.

Professor Canter dealt with the whole contract killer/ hitman issue early on in our conversation: 'The idea of meeting a stranger in a bar and slipping them an envelope under the table to go and do a hit is rather fictional. In all the cases we studied, which were about fifty, the assassin, as you're calling him, had some relationship with the person who commissioned the event. These are not necessarily hired killers who do this for a living, like in fiction. They're mates or possibly people who are under some duress from somebody else. But they have connections with whoever commissioned them. The indications are that Alistair did not know his killer... It sounds as if there was some sort of connection there... the toing and froing and the envelope, that's an interesting perspective. It's a probability, not a fact.'

He continued: 'The three shots suggest it's not an expert as well. The interesting parallel is the case of Jill Dando. She was shot with one bullet to the head, a much more clear event. The fact that he knocks on the door on a Sunday evening fits in with him seeking an opportunity to carry out this particular event, because I would have thought Alistair was vulnerable in a whole range of other situations, but an individual being sent to his house... it implies a familiarity... It begins to build up the prospect that the person who commissioned the assault had some sort of contact, there was some sort of network involved.'

I was soon to be put firmly in my place. Professor Canter relayed a quote of mine from a recent newspaper article, where I'd said, 'If you've got a why, you've got a who.' He said, 'Our approach would be more of you've got a how, you've got a who, because you may not know the reasons [for the murder], often the reasons are quite complex. The fictional idea of greed or jealousy or pride, we're all more complicated than that.'

Donna said, 'David doesn't believe in the concept of motive as a single unidimensional structure.'

The Professor added, 'That's right, we don't know why we do things. For crime fiction, you've gotta put stuff in to make it seem sensible, and for a jury, because they like a strong narrative, but the actual motives are often a great mix of things going on. Particularly, and this seems a bit of an assumption, if there are two people involved: the person who commissioned the act and the person who carried it out. It may be possible that the person who carried out the attack has some sort of vendetta that we don't know about, but even then, there would be layers of things. Had they been insulted? Were there people who saw themselves as significant and wanted to make a statement? Were they part of a criminal network and they had to demonstrate their capabilities? All these things would make motive really rather complex.'

Like me, the Professor would have liked to have had more detail about the killing – the order of shots, for example, and other details which I'd asked the police for, which had been refused. He continued, 'You should really focus on the details of what went on. Three shots with an odd weapon, up close, on a Sunday evening – all of that somehow gives a picture.'

Donna said, 'It's interactive, isn't it? Psychologically, there's a sense of somebody who's part of his world... it's a little familiar. The fact that the gunman has a negotiation with him, Alistair talks to his wife...'

'And he wants to approach him absolutely directly and look him in the eye, rather than a hit-and-run. He could have driven past on a motorbike, but that needs more skill, more weaponry,' Professor Canter added.

There's a personal quality to it as well,' Donna said.

Professor Canter concluded, 'There's a personal direct quality to it, it's almost a personal challenge...'

I asked them both to consider the information I had received that clearly implied the gunman was prepared to kill, but did not intend to kill, that he went to negotiate and not assassinate. Professor Canter wanted to know how valid this information was, so I told him it had been relayed to me via a credible source. He then said, 'It certainly fits in with what I've just said. That there was a pre-existing relationship somewhere, either the assassin or the person who sent the assassin.'

The Professor then offered a view that confirmed much of what I'd discovered: 'The other general principle you can work on in a case like this, with an intensive police investigation that's not got anywhere, the chances are that the early stages of the investigation were pretty incompetent. There is a problem there – they had the same problem with the Jill Dando case – there's so much going on at the doorstep that actually getting a clear account of what went on, exactly where the body was found, there are all those people trying to help. The ambulance people mess things up and don't really have a clear recollection of what's going on and that makes it extremely difficult.'

My mind went back to the stories I had heard of two police officers on their phones, as opposed to properly preserving the scene perhaps. The words of the Grampian Police review that said the investigation suffered 'confusion and a lack of leadership' in the early stages now seemed more pertinent than ever.

We went on to discuss the fact that Alistair Wilson was shot in the face. I was keen to hear the views of the Professor and Doctor Youngs on that. Professor Canter has spent a lot of time working with the FBI – 'They have a theory that a shot to the face is to get rid of the identity, it's a sort of insult to the person.'

Donna was quick to add, 'It's to destroy the person, not just the body, to obliterate their human identity.'

It would have been extremely helpful for all of us in assessing the potential relevance of the shot to the face and the other shots, if the police had provided the detail about the order they had been fired, exactly where they had hit Alistair Wilson, the distance they had been fired from, etcetera. Alas, we had to work with what we had. Professor Canter said, 'Presumably they can tell from the angles of the shots if Alistair was already down when he was shot in the face, or whether that was the first shot when he was standing.'

I made my frustration at the refusal of the police to provide me with that information clear.

The Professor continued, 'You could have that sort of aggressive thing, of some altercation. Say a shot to the chest, the individual falling and deciding you've got to finish them off with a shot to the face.'

We talked about the missing envelope. Then, as now, it was not entirely clear if shell casings had been recovered from the scene. I was so indebted to both the Professor and Doctor Youngs for offering up their views despite gaps in the details. Whenever they are asked by police forces to help with cases, they are supplied with every last detail. Regardless, both these renowned experts continued to offer me their invaluable opinions.

Professor Canter was clear: 'He's got some criminal history, probably in relation to serious offences. Nowadays, you have the CSI effect, where people are aware of these [forensic] issues, but somebody who had just borrowed a gun and not used it before may not be aware that there were shell cases that needed to be taken.'

Donna chimed, 'Some out-of-control testosterone-y type would not shoot someone in the face after they've gone down.'

Professor Canter was keen to know if Alistair had sustained any other injuries that might have indicated a struggle. Unfortunately, I was unable to help – I couldn't be sure if the blood Andy Burnett had seen on Alistair's hand was from a gunshot or another injury so I decided not to speculate.

Donna said, 'It's a very calm, instrumental type of killing, it's not a heated emotional interaction. It really seems like a negotiation and then this negotiation has failed therefore you're shot. He really wants him to agree to whatever he's trying to push him and persuade him and cajole him to do so.'

Professor Canter was interested in any possible vehicle that might have been used. I told them there had been no confirmed sighting of any vehicle used by the gunman. He said, 'There was no vehicle immediately present so he prepared the vehicle out of sight.'

We went on to discuss Alistair's role in the business banking section. Donna said, 'He's more likely to have things that Veronica didn't know about in his past. These people thrive on the challenge of the deal.'

We talked about Alistair leaving the bank and going to the BRE Group. Professor Canter knew a thing or two about the BRE: 'A good friend of mine worked in the BRE. Basically, they develop building regulations by doing research. The people I was in contact with were interested in behavioural science. I did a lot of work on people's behaviour in fires. Somebody with a banking background would be going into some kind of administrative role, not a scientific role. It must have been a relatively senior position they were going to give him. If he was just leaving the bank, that's really intriguing. If this was a novel, I'd say he was taking secrets from the bank and the bank wanted him to sign a non-disclosure agreement.'

As we enjoyed our dinner we talked about the reprehensible behaviour of some Bank of Scotland employees around the time Alistair was murdered.

Professor Canter said, 'The familiarity, knowing his address, doing it on a Sunday evening, not on the way to work or around the bank, would all fit, would be consistent with some dodgy connections at the bank. Possibly because he was moving on, he was going to take whatever with him and they wouldn't be able to control him anymore.'

Bob Keppel is a highly renowned former US detective and academic. He worked on the Ted Bundy serial killings and struck up a relationship with Bundy after his capture. Keppel and Professor Canter have worked together over a number of years and the Professor was keen to relay something that Keppel had told him: 'In a major investigation it's almost invariably the case that the culprit was in the police system and possibly even interviewed early on in the investigation, in the first few days. So, all the people that they looked at, that they talked to and explored, chances are that the culprit is involved.'

Professor Canter continued with his own thoughts: 'The problem with these cases that are of great public interest is the senior investigating officer is under so much pressure to deliver, it's actually very difficult for them to have a systematic overview of the situation. They do tend to grab a likely suspect and then try to find the evidence to support that. There's confirmation bias. You look for evidence to support your theory rather than looking for evidence that will challenge you. We all do it. That's why we buy the newspaper that we do, one that will confirm our world views rather than challenge our thinking.'

He continued, 'Alistair is leaving the bank... It is intriguing that the police have held so much back because it does suggest some political or commercial interest that they're very anxious to keep under wraps, so they don't get into trouble.'

We talked about the failed business venture that was Lothian House. Donna said, 'We're talking about someone whose business folds and then leaves his job, someone whose life is in disintegration.'

The Professor quickly added, 'Perhaps the bank suggested he leaves.'

We discussed the police and my dealings with them. There can be little doubt the Professor was spot on when he quipped, 'They probably think you're a bit of a pain. They have a fortress mentality.'

The full details about the envelope were yet to be revealed, but I was certain it was a coloured greetings card type envelope. This would later be confirmed by the police. The information we were theorising on was therefore right. Donna made an interesting point: 'That suggests somebody with a very cynical sense of humour.'

I told Donna and the Professor that the whole envelope aspect of this crime puzzled me deeply. If I had been the man in the black cap, I'd have shot Alistair the moment he appeared at the front door. The Professor said, 'That makes sense that he didn't intend to kill, that he handed over the envelope and expected a response. When that didn't come, he decided he had to go on to Plan B. That again suggests he's not a hired hand, an anonymous hired hand, he's somebody who is part of a process and he's able to evaluate the response that he gets, to determine whether he should kill him or not. He's got to understand what the nature of the request is.'

Donna said, 'For somebody to move from a position of negotiation to a position of killing somebody, psychologically, they're two quite different states. Unless they're very callous, genuinely psychopathic, a genuine organised criminal.'

There is no escaping the potential relevance of the notorious envelope. I asked both Donna and the Professor to consider the discussion about it between Alistair and Veronica Wilson. The Professor responded, 'The fact that Alistair would want to discuss it with his wife sort of opens up the possibility that it's not part of some totally abstract business dealings that his wife didn't know anything about. It's got to be something she could understand and it would be worth his while talking to her about. Clearly, he didn't expect to be killed or he wouldn't have gone back to the door. If these were really organised criminals, kidnapping one of the children could work, if you really needed money or something. There's got to be some process there that his killing resolves. There would have been opportunities to beat him up, if they wanted to frighten him. So, they've got to take him out of the equation.'

Donna added, 'We've done studies of serial killers and one of the styles of killing we call the execution style. It is within that style that you see the killers ensure that the person is dead. It smacks a bit of that to me.'

Professor Canter responded, 'Three shots is making sure, absolutely making sure that he's dead. It's not warning him or an angry or immediate response, it's an assassination.'

'An execution, but equally, it's not an excessive emotional killing,' said Donna.

Professor Canter added, 'There's no kicking and shouting.'

We were all frustrated that we didn't have more detail to analyse. Professor Canter again emphasised the need for knowing the order and exact placing of the shots. He would also have liked to know exactly where Alistair Wilson had stood and been found, the 'arrangement of the space' as he described it.

We'd ordered dessert and I knew Professor Canter and Dr Youngs had trains to catch. I had one burning question: 'Psychologically, where is the gunman now?'

The Professor replied, 'What these guys do, particularly in this kind of instrumental killing, is they develop justifications. We analysed the autobiographies of violent criminals and killers and there's four major justifications. It's exactly the same justifications Tony Blair gave for going into Iraq; Number one, to save yourself, kill or be killed. Number two, Honour, to show that you're respected, you don't tolerate insolence. Number three, Retribution. Victims deserved it, they had it coming to them. And number four, Collateral damage – in other words, it was an accident.'

Donna said, 'When they're not caught, they feel like they're given a second chance to construct a different life narrative so that in the end the person you're looking for can be completely unexpected.'

'So, they've constructed a completely different life?' I asked.

'Yes, in response to the offence,' said Donna.

Professor Canter added, 'The fact that they threw the gun

away also fits in with them wanting nothing more to do with it. They've got some awareness of the forensic issues but they don't want to hide the gun for some sort of future event.'

'It's just over. It implies that they think it's over, they're free. It suggests to me somebody sitting around now who has to be in an extreme state of denial. He must be thinking, I got away with it this long, nothing's going to happen now,' said Donna.

I then conjured up an image which I really didn't want to be true: 'Thirteen years on, has he got a pipe and slippers, maybe with a grandchild sitting on his knee?'

Donna replied, 'I don't know, but we've certainly seen it where a killer might want to be involved indirectly in the reopening of a case.'

The Professor added, 'He may have moved off and he may not be aware that the case has been reopened.' His next line gripped me: 'The simple rule of thumb is that it's somebody local. Most criminals don't travel very far to commit their crimes.'

I was afraid of what their response to my next question might be: 'Is he happy?'

Donna answered, 'I would say yes. He must be aware that on some level he's risked it all.'

That was not what I wanted to hear.

The Professor added, 'Some of these people, when the police eventually knock on the door, indicate a sort of relief, that they want to be caught because of their guilt. But the fact they're not caught helps their justifications, it supports their belief that they were right, that God's on their side.'

Coffee was on its way and my valuable time with these

two luminaries of investigative psychology would soon be at an end. I repeated the line about the possible motive being common knowledge among certain members of the legal profession in the Central Belt of Scotland. Did they have any thoughts on that?

The Professor responded first, 'With that sort of information, which is not in the public domain [a few days later, it would appear in the newspaper], I can see why you're in for an intriguing case. It's classic TV drama if there are some senior people keeping it under wraps.'

'It's a long time for a lot of people to have kept quiet,' Donna added.

In a perfect world I would have spent days with Professor Canter and Doctor Youngs, poring over all the information that the police would have readily given us. Alas, this was not to be the case, so as I ordered the bill and we prepared to say goodbye, I seized their concluding thoughts.

Professor Canter said, 'Alistair must have thought he was safe. Two kids in the house, going to bed, he leaves the guy at the front door…'

'As opposed to dialling 999?' I asked.

'Yep,' said the Professor.

As our coats were delivered to us, Donna had a point she wanted to reinforce: 'I'm struggling with the situation where Alistair would ask Veronica's permission or get her guidance. In my limited experience, boys aren't like that.'

Professor Canter offered up a theory, 'The police may well know who it is and they're just trying to build up the evidence.'

Their coats were on and they had trains to catch. I begged

the Professor for his final thoughts on motive: 'Don't get too distracted by looking at the victim for a motive. Sometimes there can be a significant event in the life of the offender which drives them down a particular route of offending.'

I gave them both my sincere thanks for finding the time to meet me and then they were gone. Back at the table, I ordered a glass of wine – I wanted some time to mull over what I had just learned. I've gone over their words time and time again. I know that when this murderer is finally caught, much of what they said will undoubtedly apply.

If Police Scotland would like to engage the Professor and the Doctor to do a full and thorough examination of the case, and I think they should, they should get in touch.

CHAPTER NINETEEN

A NEW SOURCE

It was November 2017. The thirteenth anniversary of Alistair Wilson's murder was looming. I knew there would be a significant amount of publicity this time around. Professor Wilson and I had both been commenting on the crime and getting lots of airtime and column inches. You didn't have to be Einstein to work out that the police were going to crank up their media machine; I also had a plan.

So, I contacted my source who had given me the Livingston FC information. I asked the source to run the information by me once again, to see if there was anything else they recalled, or if there was any flesh we could put on what were fairly bare but very interesting bones. Deep down, I was hoping the source's contact may have had a change of heart and would now speak to me directly. My source said, 'The person who told me the information will not go on record because he doesn't want someone coming to his doorstep, like they did

Alistair. You should look back to when Livingston Football Club went bankrupt. Alistair's banker boss was supposed to be making money from the deal. The hitman was sent to scare Alistair, but it went wrong.'

I felt I could now approach the newspaper that I had dealt with a few weeks earlier when I'd given them the exclusive about this new potential motive. I hadn't declared then what the potential motive was, and I wasn't about to do so now, but I thought I could give them three strands that might make a story, while keeping the Livingston FC information under wraps. For my pitch I broke these strands down into easily digestible soundbites: (1) The gunman did not intend to shoot Alistair, he went to negotiate rather than assassinate (I'd heard that twice now, albeit from the same source); (2) The motive for Alistair's murder is common knowledge among many in the legal profession in the Central Belt, and (3) The reason those people who know the motive won't speak up is because they're scared.

The newspaper went for it. They sent a journalist down from Scotland. I met him at my local train station and we came back to my house for a few hours. We got on very well, although as you would expect from a seasoned pro, he did probe away to see if he could tease anything more out of me. Once our business was out of the way, we went for a bite to eat and I dropped him back at the station. The newspaper was happy: they had more than enough information around which to construct a spread in the Sunday edition, which would hit the shelves two days before the anniversary, 26 November. I had more people to see in Nairn and other research to do so it made sense for me to be in town the day the article was published. I would also be in Nairn for the anniversary, when awareness of the case would undoubtedly be heightened.

My ever-frugal wife made the bookings because she was convinced she could get the flight, car hire and accommodation cheaper than I had last time around. As always, she was right: she came in nearly £300 cheaper than I'd paid for my October visit. When we factored in the cash the newspaper was going to pay me, I reckoned there would be enough money left in the kitty for yet another trip to Nairn in 2018, should I need it.

In the run-up to this trip my attention had been drawn to a family who lived close to Alistair Wilson at the time of the murder. The information was sketchy but I wouldn't be in Nairn long before the phone would start to ring.

I arrived in Nairn late afternoon on Sunday, 26 November. This time I was staying at The Braeval Hotel in Crescent Road. It was where Andy Burnett had been when he heard about the shooting and where I had been given the 'in-house' line in the bathroom, back in 2009. As usual, I made some phone calls to let people know I was in town. The police were not on my list of people to notify, they'd made their position perfectly clear. As I walked to the Fishertown part of Nairn, I took the opportunity to push flyers through doors as I went. That night I had an enjoyable dinner and a glass of wine with a couple of people who had become friends in recent years, who were keen to hear of my progress. I told them what I could and tasked them to do some digging for me. We said our goodbyes and I returned to The Braeval.

The bar of The Braeval has an astonishing selection of whiskies, many of which I've never heard of. After treating myself to a nightcap, I toddled off to bed.

I was up bright and early the following day, which was just as well. As soon as I opened my eyes, I turned on the TV and saw that Police Scotland and Veronica Wilson had staged their media splash for the day before the anniversary. Alistair's murder was the main story and the segments were being repeated throughout the morning on the breakfast programme; the case was getting a lot of airtime.

Veronica may not have wanted to speak to me, but she was not shy about talking to the BBC. In a recorded interview she spoke of the need for herself and the boys to know why her husband had been killed: 'A who and why would just make such a difference to us being able to move on.' She continued, 'It's harder the older the boys get. Obviously, when they were little, they were just told their dad had died, and he wasn't there anymore. They're young men now so they just can't understand it. Why somebody would do it to their dad and why somebody's not been caught. Justice is a huge factor and issue that they have.'

She went on to say that mistaken identity is 'the only thing that makes sense to me,' before adding, 'I believe I did know Alistair and that evening, he did have the choice not to go back down. So, I believe that he didn't know. If he'd survived, he still couldn't have told us anymore, so the only thing that makes any sense to me was that it was the wrong Alistair Wilson. We didn't have any sort of lifestyle that there was ever any threat. I couldn't even imagine why people are actually killed. You know, you see things, other people, and you just presume there's something dark or sinister in their life. But I knew Alistair inside out and there was nothing there.'

Here, I feel compelled to point out the obvious: Veronica did not go to work with her husband.

After thirteen long years, Police Scotland finally decided to tell all about the envelope. A suitably stern-faced Detective Superintendent Gary Cunningham, who was now leading the investigation, was pictured onscreen holding an unmistakably blue envelope. This was not an A4 envelope, as described by certain media outlets many years previously, but a greetings card envelope. We were told that the envelope was empty and it was confirmed that the name 'Paul' was on it. One can only wonder why it took the police so long to release this information. As part of this media splash Cunningham had previously met journalists and during questioning, he said he 'cannot rule out' that Alistair Wilson's murder was a case of mistaken identity, that the envelope may have been a distraction device, or that the killer may have expected something to be put inside it.

The police also revealed that a weapon identical to the one used to kill Alistair had been handed in to them in 2016. This gun had apparently been found during a house clearance. The occupier of the house had been an old man who had gone into a care home. Apparently, this man had been a prisoner of war during World War Two and the gun was believed to be a trophy brought back from the conflict. We were told that only thirteen of this type of weapon had been recovered in the UK since 2008. Bearing in mind how quickly and easily my contact Sam had been able to source the weapon that I had handled, maybe they are more common in the Highlands than originally thought. Another similar weapon of the same calibre had also been handed to police in 2016.

This was a Belgian-made Melior pistol surrendered by an old man during an air rifle amnesty. I was beginning to think there might be more handguns in Nairn than in my part of Southeast London.

DS Cunningham appealed to the public: 'I need to know if they have any ideas who "Paul" is. And I need to know if there's any ideas as to why this envelope contained nothing.'

The interview of Veronica Wilson and the other clips were repeated not only on the breakfast programme but on other news bulletins throughout the day. Alistair Wilson's murder was the talk of the town. Good! Sources were calling me to make sure I'd been watching. I already knew that the police had been busying themselves in Nairn in recent weeks, revisiting witnesses and interviewing other people they thought might be of interest, and my sources reconfirmed this. I was delighted – the more resources the police were allocating to the case, the better. A picture was being painted that was very different to 2009 when the police admitted there wasn't even an inquiry team.

I wondered if the publicity that I had garnered recently had played a part or had any influence in all of this. Professor David Wilson had also been commenting widely on the crime and he is not a man to be ignored. Maybe the police were reinvigorated out of their own sense of duty, but it is an unmistakable fact that media pressure does influence police investigations. A vastly experienced murder detective admitted to me that if a relative puts pressure on the police, if an MP gets on board a case, or if there's a lot of coverage in the media, then the police will respond; they will react.

During one of my trips to Nairn, a reliable source told me

an interesting story about a possible sighting of Alistair Wilson on Friday, 26 November 2004, a mere two days before he was shot. A few days after the murder, this source was queuing at Nairn police station to give a statement about his association with Alistair. Standing in front of him were two men who, judging from the type and state of their clothes, appeared to be builders. When these two men started talking to the officer at the front counter the source could clearly overhear what they were saying. They told police that the previous Friday they had been in a betting shop in Nairn High Street. They noticed a man who looked a bit out of place because he was smartly dressed in a suit. He was placing very large bets, so large, in fact, that they tried to find out what horses this man was backing, because they thought they should back the same ones. After Alistair's murder they had seen pictures of him in the media and recognised him as the man in the bookies.

The bookmakers are no longer there, unfortunately. I appealed via Twitter and my Facebook page on Alistair Wilson's murder for these men to come forward but have heard nothing. I've tasked other sources to try and locate them but have drawn a blank. Please exercise caution around this possible sighting as I have not been able to confirm it. If true, it could potentially be highly significant. And if you were one of those men in the bookies, please get in touch, I'd very much like to talk to you.

A number of people had been working for me behind the scenes, covertly, quietly, almost in an undercover way. I am so grateful to these wonderful people. I don't pay them – the most they might get from me is a coffee and a scone, or a beer or maybe dinner. They never ask me for anything. One enquired of me if the police or the charity Crimestoppers were still offering a reward, which they're not. Overwhelmingly, they just want to see justice. Consequently, it came as no surprise when I received a text during this trip giving me instructions to a meeting point. I was to meet a potentially new source. This meeting had been facilitated by an intermediary. When the time came, I jumped in my hire car and followed the directions.

These directions took me way out of town into a very rural area. Eventually, I went over a bridge and pulled into a small layby, where I was instructed to park. And then I waited. It was like the good old bad old days working undercover, except I'm now a lot longer in the tooth. Way off the beaten track, I was highly unlikely to be spotted by anybody. I'll admit to feeling a wee bit tense.

Eventually, my new source arrived. I got out of my car, walked casually towards him and we shook hands. I'd worn a robust winter coat and a pair of North Face boots, which he immediately commented favourably on. That was a good ice-breaker. If I'd turned up in townie shoes and a blazer, I don't think he'd have been quite so willing to engage. I followed him as he strode purposefully into the dense woods. This was a man clearly at home in such a rugged environment. I watched my footing and did my utmost not to go base over apex; I did not want to make a fool of myself.

A network of names and associates emerged, with tales of alleged admissions, gossip, rumour and intrigue. I had a lot more work to do.

CHAPTER TWENTY

THE DOUGLAS FAMILY

I have always listened to anybody who wants to talk to me about Alistair Wilson's murder. With my phone number and email address available to anybody determined enough to find them, it may come as no surprise to hear that many people have reached out with a theory or some information that they think is valid. My social media profiles have also been a way in which people have been able to enter into dialogue with me. If they take the time to speak to me, it is only right that I pay them the common courtesy of listening.

Some of what I've heard has sounded quite fanciful but whenever possible, I have tried to corroborate the information. One caller told me a rather elaborate and convoluted story about a function at a golf club that resulted in a female member of staff being raped. The caller claimed Alistair Wilson was involved in the 'rape' and that this was the motive for him being shot. Knowing what I do about Alistair,

I struggle to think of a more unlikely scenario. Even though I am convinced beyond doubt that this version of events is complete poppycock, I listened to everything the caller had to say. I even visited the golf club mentioned, but perhaps not surprisingly, no one had any recollection of any such event.

I'm sure these people believe that what they are telling me is true, but when there isn't a shred of corroborating evidence, I have to set their views aside. Being deluged with these tales is a hazard of doing what I do. The police have more time and resources to bottom these stories out, although that of course must sometimes be frustrating. I'm convinced that some of the people who have contacted me have mental health issues, so I have to proceed respectfully and with caution. I don't think anybody has deliberately contacted me with a view to wasting my time.

Another caller contacted me to say that back in 2004, he had a raging cocaine habit and sourced his drugs from a dealer in Inverness named Paul. This dealer was apparently a man of violence and the former user felt this particular Paul could have been capable of murder. Now I don't doubt for a moment that what the caller was saying was true, but there has never been a shred of evidence, gossip or rumour linking Alistair to drugs, so I thanked the man for getting in touch and sat on that information. I certainly wasn't about to disappear off into the Inverness drugs underworld, looking for Paul. Don't get me wrong, I most certainly would have done so, had I thought it might have moved my research forward, but I didn't, so I didn't.

One Sunday, I was at home and about to sit down with my family for a Mother's Day lunch, when my phone rang: it was a withheld number. A man who wouldn't give me his name rabbited on for over half an hour, during which he repeatedly told me that he knew the identity of the gunman. At one point he was 100 per cent sure that he knew who the killer was, at another point in the conversation, he was 101 per cent sure. What became clear to me, however, was that this man was theorising, as opposed to being in the know. After doing the bulk of the listening, I asked him outright who pulled the trigger. But he didn't tell me – he was far more interested in asking about reward money and I told him there wasn't any. He told me then he had spoken to the police many years ago and not heard back from them, something which still irritated him.

I felt a bit sorry for this man because it was clear from what he told me that the crime still played heavily on his mind. With the gravy congealing and my family getting irritated by my absence from the dinner table, I assured this troubled soul that I would take his call anytime he chose to tell me who shot Alistair. I haven't heard from him since.

I'll always listen to people's theories; they are often extremely interesting. If you have one, please get in touch. Gossip is sometimes good, I'm all ears. And I'm a firm believer that rumour is often truth's lubricant. After all, it was gossip and rumour that took me down the next line of inquiry. It had all been started by that meeting in the woods.

As a result of what I'd been told as I clambered through the woodland, I started to take a look at the Douglas family. Around 1974, James Keith Douglas (known to everybody as Keith) and his wife Theresa (Terry) moved to Nairn from Bradford. They had four children; two daughters, followed by two sons: Paul Craig Douglas (known to everybody as Craig) and the youngest, Shaun. Craig is now aged fifty-one; Shaun is some three years younger. The eldest daughter has lived her entire adult life in Bradford, but sadly, the younger daughter died of cancer in 2016, aged just fifty-four.

Cancer also claimed Terry's life in 2000.

By talking to those who knew them, I started to build up a picture of Craig and Shaun. I then spoke to a local man who had known them for many years – I'll call him Bruce.

Bruce opened up by saying, 'Shaun has always been a strange one. Craig is a *Jackanory* one. If you've been shipwrecked, he's been sunk.' Bruce hadn't seen either of them for some years, 'Craig made up stories. Shaun was a bit of a nutter.' Bruce told me that Shaun had hung around with a man who ran a halfway house in Inverness, which provided accommodation for people recently released from prison. Clearly I had to be very careful about this uncorroborated information. I needed to speak to Craig.

Before that could happen, an intermediary smoothed the way for me to speak to Keith Douglas, the boys' father, who still lived in the family home in Nairn. I'd been given his phone number; his house was a mere 155 paces from Alistair Wilson's front door – I know that because I've walked the short route time and time again. So, I parked my car close to Keith's house, in a position where I could see his front door, and I called him. He told me it was fine to come round; I said I would be with him in a matter of seconds. I started walking towards his house, all the while keeping an eye on the front door. Almost immediately after I'd hung up, a blonde woman came hurtling out of Keith's front door and jumped in a vehicle parked immediately outside; the vehicle sped off. I can fully understand that not everybody wants to be seen by me nor to speak to me, but I still thought it a little strange. The old-school detective in me that will never leave ensured that I wrote down the registration number of her car, just in case. I knocked on the door and Keith invited me in.

It was a substantial house set on three floors. We climbed the stairs to a lounge on the first floor. The dying embers of a log fire just about kept the chill away. An offer to put the kettle on never came, although Keith was otherwise welcoming. He started by explaining that he had recently had a fall down a stone staircase and consequently, his memory was not what it used to be. He told me he was eighty-two years old. Despite living in Nairn for the past forty-three years, he retains a strong and proud Yorkshire accent. It soon became clear my interest in the Douglas family was shared by others.

Keith explained that two or three weeks earlier, a pair of police detectives who were working on the Alistair Wilson case had come to his house. They had asked Keith to detail his life history in depth. The same officers had apparently been to interview his son Craig a couple of weeks earlier. So, now I had a bit of a dilemma: should I inform the police of my interest in the Douglas family? But I answered my own question with a resolute no.

Keith worked as a joiner all his life. He travelled wherever his work took him: Holland, Germany, France and most major UK cities. He has the bulbous, toughened hands of a man who has held tools all his working life and he took delight in showing me some of the incredible carpentry work that he's carried out on his home: gigantic oak doors, beamed ceilings and inventive storage solutions all adorn the place, which has seven bedrooms and three lounges. The house had previously been described to me as the sort of home where you might not see a fellow resident for two days because it was so big – I now knew what that person meant.

Many years ago, Keith and his wife Terry had let some of their rooms as bed-and-breakfast for men working on nearby oil rigs. When the rigs disappeared, they continued to provide B&B to holidaymakers, but in the end, as Keith said, 'It weren't worth the while.'

I asked him about his son Shaun. Keith said that as a child, Shaun was 'an awkward little bugger' and that Terry 'couldn't control him like she should have done'. It appeared the mainstream school in Nairn couldn't control Shaun either, so he was sent away to what was then known as a 'special school' for pupils with social, educational and behavioural needs called Raddery, which was on the Black Isle.

Raddery was run by a couple who made a point of visiting Keith and Terry before Shaun was admitted. The school was residential so he would only return home maybe once a month or during the school holidays. Keith heaped praise on Raddery: 'I tell you what, they learnt him. He come away from there knowledgeable. He come away a different lad altogether and he were brainy, that were the thing I liked about it. When he come away from there, he were on his way, clever. As time's gone by, he's got better and better. When you talk to him, you can tell he's knowledgeable.'

Keith now lived alone because Shaun had apparently met a woman online and moved to Canada to be with her. That was five or six years ago, according to Keith. Shaun had only phoned his father three times since moving away. Keith didn't have a phone number or an address for his son and details about his current location were a bit patchy: 'All I know is he got involved with this lass. Apparently, she comes from a good family. Her mother and father are well up in running the town. It's Fairbanks. To get to Fairbanks, you need to get a plane. This plane takes about an hour, it's virtually on the Arctic Circle. There's not an airport, just a landing strip… You can get there by boat, but it takes two days.'

Keith explained that only thirty families live in the settlement where Shaun and his partner were living and these families are mainly Eskimos and Canadian-Indians: 'The Eskimos have shown Shaun how to kill walrus, how to cook it. Or find a stag, shoot it. If you want fish for a change, you can catch a salmon. No problem, that's your tea. I think they've moved off. Last time I spoke to him, he was in New York, end of story.'

I asked Keith to cast his mind back to the night Alistair Wilson was murdered. He told me that Craig was married and living in Ardersier, some six miles from Nairn, up the A96. Keith was apparently watching television in a lounge on the ground floor and Shaun was in his bedroom on the second floor. Keith explained, 'I never heard a thing. The next morning, at seven o'clock, I went to get my paper and scarper [to work]. I seen the [barrier] tape and two policewomen. Somebody said, "There's been a murder, somebody shot him." First I knew about it.

'Some three or four days later, a detective came asking me questions: "Where were you that night?" I told him, "Sat here, watching telly." He said, "You've got two sons, haven't you?"

I said, "What have they got to do with it?" He said, "Well, I've got to get it all down on paper." So, I said my youngest son were upstairs in bed. He said, "Can I come back and have a word with your son?" I says, "Come back whenever you did." [I assumed by this he meant 'Come back whenever you like.'] It were two months after when he come back, Shaun weren't in. The detective never came again. But this couple [of detectives] recently went right through my working life. And Craig, where's Craig? The police have been to see him. They wanted to know where Shaun were. I said Canada, Northern Canada.'

If Keith Douglas's recollection of events is true and accurate, and I have no reason to suggest they're not, then once again I've discovered another major error by the Northern Constabulary. Shaun, a single local man, who was in his mid-thirties at the time of the murder, and who I've been told was a bit of a loner, was not interviewed by detectives. Clearly he should have been as part of routine house-to-house inquiries. From what Keith told me, it appeared that Police Scotland were certainly interested in both Shaun and Craig, some thirteen years after the murder. I know hindsight is a wonderful thing, but investigating a major crime is so often about the detail, dotting every 'i' and crossing every 't'. It would appear the Northern Constabulary were not as thorough as they should have been. Could they have been fixated on another theory or line of inquiry and were therefore ploughing all their efforts into that?

Keith confirmed that Craig was christened Paul Craig. I asked if anybody ever called him 'Paul': 'Might have done years ago.' As Keith showed me to the front door, he showed me the ground-floor lounge, where he had been watching TV on the night of the murder. It was almost adjacent to the front door.

Keith said, 'He [Shaun] couldn't have shot him cos he'd have to walk past this lounge, where I were watching telly.'

'You do have a back door, though, don't you?' I said.

Keith's reply was short: 'Aye.'

We left on good terms. Keith is keen to see justice: 'I wish they'd hurry up and get who it were. It's now't to do with me.'

Speaking to Shaun and Craig Douglas now became a priority. The trouble was, if Shaun was in some remote part of Canada, that might prove rather challenging. I quietly hoped he was now based in New York, working, paying taxes and using social media, so he would therefore pop up on an accessible database of some description.

A friend of mine who worked in the intelligence gathering world was based in North America. I gave her what little information I had. She would have liked more information than I could give her. Ever the professional, she vowed to forge ahead as best she could. She contacted me a couple of days later to tell me that Shaun Douglas was quite a common name in America and Canada, but she was in the process of trying to narrow down her list of names to the most likely matches. If we managed to track down the Shaun Douglas we were looking for, I told her I was perfectly willing to get on a plane and get in front of him.

Meanwhile, Keith's information about Craig's location had been a bit more helpful. I now knew Craig was living and working on the estate of a wealthy landowner somewhere in Scotland, probably a couple of hours' car journey from

Nairn. An address or a phone number would clearly have been a great help, but regardless, I tasked some of my sources in Nairn and a firm of private investigators to do their thing. A couple of weeks later, I was provided with a landline number for Craig. I've subsequently had a number of phone conversations with him. His answers to my questions have always been consistent.

The following is an amalgamation of what he has told me during those conversations: Craig and Shaun were young boys when their family relocated from Yorkshire to Nairn. Life at school was apparently difficult for both boys because they were English and suffered taunting and worse from the local children. Craig said that the taunting signalled the end of his education as he spent the following years at school 'defending myself'. He left with no qualifications. Craig told me that when Shaun was about twelve or thirteen, he assaulted a teacher and that was the catalyst for him being sent away to Raddery.

As kids, the pair never got on. Craig says they 'fought like hell, we were always at each other's throats'. As he grew older and started work (as a driver, machine operator or as a doorman in pubs in the town), he would conceal money in the family home, in case he wanted to go away on holiday with his mates or buy a motorbike, or whatever else took his fancy. Craig alleged that Shaun would find this money and steal it: 'He started digging into my pocket, taking money from my wallet, money that I'd saved, that I had stashed in the house. I thought he'd never find it, but he did. Cost me thousands in the long run. That didn't go down too good. I lost the rag and got hold of him, give him a clout or two.'

Craig was in his late teens at this stage, Shaun was three years younger.

He continued: 'I don't know what he spent it on. I don't know if it went up in smoke or up his nose. I'd say this guy's got no respect for nobody. He'd then go and hide for a while.'

Craig recalls how he'd warn his brother about stealing from him: 'Stay out of my room, stay out of my life, but if you keep doing this, I'm going to get severely fucking pissed off!' Thereafter, 'We didn't used to see each other much.'

Just as well, I thought.

Craig had his troubles as a young man. There was dope smoking, cocaine and amphetamines: 'I made quite a few enemies, I got in a bit of bother. I got roped into things.' He avoided prison but paid a few fines: 'I had a lot of trouble when I was younger cos people didn't like me, I used to get the blame a lot. Then the police would be at my door. Anything that happened in town, like fights in pubs, the finger would get pointed at me. It used to send me bonkers, like. Then I'd go looking for revenge. Then you'd think to yourself, Jesus, get a life!'

Craig did just that: he got treatment for his heavy drinking and has not touched a drop of alcohol in over twenty years. He moved away from Nairn to Ardersier. Then he married, bought a house and had a child. Unfortunately, the marriage did not last. He was living in the marital home at the time of Alistair Wilson's murder. I asked if he had known Alistair: 'I probably spoke to him in the pub,' he told me, but he could not elaborate beyond that.

Craig was keen to give me his opinion of his little brother: 'Shaun's Shaun. He's quiet. Everybody thinks he's strange cos he's quiet. He just lives in his own world, really. He sleeps all day and lives by night. He's at the computer, all that kind of thing… He's very quiet, very deep, he'll tell you nothing. I don't know what makes him tick.'

Craig now lives in a tiny hamlet consisting of six houses. There's no pub and no shop for twelve miles: 'It suits me down to the ground.' It was here that two detectives investigating Alistair Wilson's murder came to interview him in the summer of 2017. Among the many, many questions they asked during a visit that lasted some three hours were, 'Do you think it was your brother?' and 'Do you think he was capable of it?' Craig said he gave answers identical to the ones he'd given me.

He then told me that the cops 'were on the edge of their seats' when they said a name was on the envelope. They then told Craig, 'Your name is on the envelope – Paul.' Puzzled, he asked the cops, 'How did my name end up on the envelope?' He explained to the detectives that he had been known to everybody as 'Craig' since he came to Scotland. There had apparently been three or four Pauls in his school class, so Craig told the teacher that the only name he would respond to was Craig. That did the trick, the name stuck.

At one point during his questioning the detectives reeled off a list of names and asked Craig whether he knew these people. Some of the names were Russian or Polish sounding and he told them, 'I don't know any foreigners.' Other names he did recognise; one in particular stood out. It was a man who Craig said was, 'Handy with his fists and his feet and would take things too far. He used to do a lot of stuff that was totally fucking bonkers.' This man's propensity for violence could sometimes result in 'severe injuries for someone. He was always up to some kind of shite.' Apparently, rumours abounded, including one that did the rounds, saying this man's father was a freemason and that was why he never faced any form of legal sanction. According to Craig, this man 'liked making people's lives a misery', yet he didn't seem to face any consequences for his actions. Craig mentioned this to the detectives and asked, 'How come nothing ever happened?' He was astonished by the response he got from one of the officers: 'Cos he's a grass, Craig. Always has been.'

I was flabbergasted when I heard this. That's why I've repeatedly asked Craig to retell this part of his story and his recollection is always unwavering and unchanging.

Snitches get stitches – I suspect most of us have heard that expression. They sometimes get a lot worse. Two informants that I dealt with both ended up being shot dead. They lived and operated in the world of international drug dealing and other serious crime, rather than small town violence and associated gossip and rumour. I'm convinced they also got up to other criminal activity that we didn't get to hear about. They were warned; they were told repeatedly not to engage in crime, but we couldn't be with them twenty-four hours a day.

Informants are odious, unscrupulous people. Most would sell their granny down the road if there was a few quid in it for them. I certainly did not associate with them when I was off-duty, unlike some of my colleagues. Handling informants is a challenging and often difficult thing to do: you must be firm, incorruptible and beyond reproach. They are snakes, but they're very necessary in the fight against crime. It's a filthy, dirty, murky and often complex world of criminality out there. Informants save time, money and effort, and they often pass on information that the police would not obtain in any other way. They most definitely need protecting.

You don't have to be a top-echelon gangster to end up facing retribution for being a police informant. For many involved in criminality, there is no greater sin than being a grass. In my opinion for a police officer to confirm to a member of the public that a particular person is an informant is an act of gross misconduct: informants' identities should remain secret for reasons blatantly obvious to us all. What if Craig Douglas still harboured a deep-seated and longstanding grudge against the man who always seemed to get away with stuff, who he now knows courtesy of Police Scotland, was an informant? He could now exact his own retribution or spread the word far and wide that the man was a grass and let someone else do the dirty work. Fortunately, that is unlikely because Craig has left his tearaway days far behind him.

There will more than likely be others out there who still harbour bad feelings towards this man. Have the police confirmed to anybody else that he was an informant? If anything happens to this man from here on in, the police may have only themselves to blame. The disclosure of his role as a police informant is utterly unforgivable. If Craig is telling the truth, Police Scotland has a lot to answer for.

Craig told me that the detectives told him, 'We're getting places with it,' meaning the investigation into Alistair Wilson's murder. They also warned, 'You might not have seen the last of us.' With a clear conscience, he replied, 'There's no blood on my hands.'

He told me he had last seen his brother Shaun sometime

around the beginning of 2017 in Nairn – 'Just a short bump into, say hello and cheerio sort of thing, don't get no long-term conversations between us.' If this sighting was true, perhaps Shaun had returned from North America permanently.

I needed to ring Keith Douglas. Meanwhile, I tasked my Nairn sources to keep their eyes and ears open, I still wanted to speak to Shaun himself. I didn't have long to wait before information about him came my way. A source called to say they had recently seen Shaun in a car with his dad.

Once again, Keith appeared happy to talk. In fact, we've had a few phone conversations since I first met him at his house. He confirmed that Shaun had been staying with him, but on a fairly ad hoc basis: 'He's trying to get a job, there's not much about. He kept going away for a couple of days, then come waltzing back in.' It seems Keith has made it clear to Shaun that both me and the police want to speak to him: 'The police called last week, I haven't seen him since.' Shaun has apparently taken advice from a solicitor, who has advised his client he doesn't have to talk to the police. He made his views about the police clear to his dad: 'They'll be twisting it and turning it, and I'll go to prison.'

Keith told me, 'Your book has got up his nose.' So be it. I'm on a search for the truth and if somebody the police and I both want to talk to gets upset with me writing a book, then tough.

Shaun might have a point when he talks about 'twisting' and 'turning'. Two of the most notable cases of recent times both had suspects that the police appeared determined to prove were guilty when conclusive and irrefutable evidence simply wasn't there. Both lived close to the scene of the crimes and I'm sure they won't take offence when I say some may have regarded them as a little strange…

CHAPTER TWENTY-ONE

FIT-UPS AND FUCK-UPS

On Wednesday, 15 July 1992, twenty-three-year-old Rachel Nickell was walking on Wimbledon Common in south-west London. Her two-year-old son, Alex, was by her side. She was brutally attacked in an act of savage wickedness. Fatally stabbed and sexually assaulted, she was found by a passer-by, who spotted Alex clinging to his mother's lifeless body.

A psychologist was drafted in to assist the police investigation and he drew up an offender profile. The police decided that a single man living alone nearby fitted their profile. His name was Colin Stagg. It was decided to launch an undercover operation, where an attractive female officer would befriend Stagg, in the hope that he might confess to her that he had killed Rachel.

Around then I was at the peak of my powers as an undercover cop. I knew the undercover officer who was selected for this role; she went by the codename of 'Lizzie James'. I also knew a number of the detectives working on the case. When I bumped into one of them at Scotland Yard, we went for coffee in the canteen. Rachel Nickell's murder was incredibly high-profile at the time so I asked him how the investigation was going. He was convinced they had got their man in Colin Stagg, although at the time they didn't have the evidence to charge him. There was no altering his view; he wouldn't countenance any other possible theory or line of inquiry whatsoever. As far as he was concerned, Stagg was the killer and they were going to prove it.

The undercover operation lasted several months. Eventually, even though there hadn't been a full and frank confession by Stagg to Lizzie James, the decision was taken to charge him. The 1994 trial was as high-profile as the investigation and the case collapsed through lack of evidence. The undercover operation drew some scathing criticism from the judge, Mr Justice Ognall, who said the police had used 'deceptive conduct of the grossest kind'.

I was in the office of the undercover unit at Scotland Yard that afternoon and watched the Detective Chief Inspector running around like a headless chicken as he tried to deal with the fallout. He was frantically fielding phone calls, summonsing people to his office and preparing answers for some senior officers, who were clearly very unhappy with the criticism the undercover operation had attracted. The embattled DCI was predicting that this was the end of undercover work as we knew it. It wasn't, of course: he was just a bit panic stricken and in fear of the mother of all rollockings that was soon to come his way.

In 2008, Rachel Nickell's killer, convicted sex attacker and murderer Robert Napper, appeared at the Old Bailey, charged with her murder. He pleaded guilty to manslaughter on the grounds of diminished responsibility. He will never taste freedom. Some years ago I was having a drink with one of my wife's former police bosses. He told me that he'd rung the original murder inquiry team and told them to take a long, close look at Napper; he'd been ignored.

Numerous inquiries and hearings stemmed from this tragic case and the flawed investigation into it. Colin Stagg received over £700,000 in compensation from the police but told the press in 2017 that he'd spent every penny on luxury cars, expensive holidays, guitars and bad investments. All in attempt to apparently make up for lost time, blighted by his imprisonment and the stench of suspicion that lingered around him. Lizzie James's police career was brought to a premature end, as were the careers of others: there were no winners.

The Jill Dando case has been mentioned before within these pages. Both Professor Wilson and Professor Canter made reference to it in my conversations with them. At the time of her death, Jill was one of the most recognisable faces in the land. She worked for the BBC, presenting the news, *The Holiday Programme* and *Crimewatch*.

On Monday, 26 April 1999, at around 11.30 a.m. and in broad daylight, she was shot dead with a single 9mm bullet to the head, on the front doorstep of her home in Fulham, south-west London. It was rare for Jill to visit her home address at that time because she spent most of her downtime at the home of her fiancé, Alan Farthing. There were very few witnesses to her murder. Understandably the case attracted enormous media interest and many theories as to who was responsible were put forward.

My personal view is that whoever was responsible must have had advance knowledge of Jill's movements, or her 'pattern of life' to quote a surveillance term. If a gunman were to loiter endlessly in a residential street, armed, waiting and hoping his prey would arrive, then he is taking an enormous risk of being spotted and creating alarm among those who would see him. While I have not yet studied this case in depth, I am sure the killer must have had the resources and skills to have either carried out surveillance on Jill Dando or her home address, or they had otherwise had access to information that would inform them of her movements. Failing that, they had an incredible amount of luck to have been lying in wait at just the right time, as she arrived at her home.

The police took a long, hard look at a man who lived nearby, who at a later trial would be described by his own lawyers as 'The local nutter'. Barry George lived alone and had a particularly low IQ of 75, putting him in the lowest 5 per cent of the population. He had come to the police's attention in the past. In May 2000 he was arrested and charged with Jill Dando's murder. At his initial trial the prosecution alleged that Barry George was obsessed with guns, celebrities and stalking women. Forensic evidence was produced, most notably a tiny speck of what may have been firearms' residue found in the pocket of a coat belonging to George. In 2001, he was convicted of murdering Jill and sentenced to life imprisonment.

But Barry George had a resolute and determined sister

called Michelle Diskin, who was always convinced of her brother's innocence. Two appeals followed. Eventually, his original conviction for murder was set aside and a retrial ordered. This took place in 2008. The forensic evidence surrounding the speck of what may have been firearms' residue, which had played such a central role during George's original trial, was not heard by the jury because of doubts surrounding its reliability. Much of the remaining evidence was circumstantial – for example, the jury were told that George had claimed to be the cousin of Freddie Mercury, the late and great lead singer of Queen. He wasn't. George has also claimed to be in the SAS. This was mere fantasy. Over two thousand photographs of women had been found in George's flat. It was claimed he had taken these photographs and this was all part of his stalking behaviour. Before his original arrest, George had been kept under surveillance by the police for three weeks and had been seen to approach a number of women, trying to spark a conversation with them. Police had also found a holster and military magazines and a picture of George wearing a gas mask and holding a starting pistol.

The defence argued throughout that Barry George was incapable of carrying out a crime as sophisticated as the murder of Jill Dando.

The trial lasted eight weeks. It took the jury less than two days to acquit Barry George of murder. After eight long years in jail, he was released and sped away from court in a taxi, pursued by a gaggle of photographers.

Commander Simon Foy from the Metropolitan Police expressed disappointment at the verdict and said the police would be 'reflecting upon it'. As I write this, ten years on, if you go to the Metropolitan Police website and type 'Jill Dando' into the search bar, you will draw a blank. My guess would be that no detectives are currently working on the case.

CHAPTER TWENTY-TWO

A KILLER IN CONTROL

I was in my office at home. Actually, the term 'office' is a bit grandiose. It's our spare bedroom, little more than a box into which you could squeeze a single bed and not much else. My desk, chair, printer and some drawers are all rammed in snugly. A set of shelves which I miraculously managed to put together without inflicting serious injury upon myself ensure every scrap of space is utilised. Far from luxurious or glamorous, but it works for me.

It was December 2017. The thirteenth anniversary of Alistair Wilson's murder had been and gone, so the information about the size, colour and the name on the infamous envelope was now common knowledge. We had also been informed by the police that the envelope was empty, unopened and hadn't contained anything. None of this information had been available when I'd met with Professor Canter and Dr Youngs.

I reached out to Professor David Wilson, the renowned

authority on criminology, whose work I featured earlier. To my absolute delight, he responded. We had a conversation on the phone and discussed our mutual interest in Alistair Wilson's murder. I was thrilled and delighted that he generously agreed to give up some of his time to meet me. It was only right that I travelled to him, so as soon as our call was over, I booked my train ticket.

Over the years I've spoken to journalists and people in TV who have claimed they don't really know what criminology is. For clarity and the avoidance of any doubt, I thought I'd include an authoritative definition here.

Criminology is a social science and is sometimes called a 'rendezvous discipline' as it has roots in Psychology, Sociology, Law, Philosophy and even History, Geography and Politics. However, at a very basic level, criminologists are interested in the scientific study of crime and how different societies will deal with the problems that crime and offenders create in their communities. They are also interested in solutions to crime and how different approaches – such as punishment, policing and the criminal justice system more broadly – might change the behaviour of offenders. In order to do this, criminologists study the behaviour of offenders, none more so than Professor Wilson.

Some days later, I emerged from Birmingham New Street station as excited as a child on his way to the sweet shop. I've long admired Professor Wilson's work and his achievements and I was trying to remain dignified as the heightened anticipation coursed through me. I appreciate that some people might idolise sports stars, movie stars or pop stars, but to me, people like Professor Wilson are rock'n'roll! A few minutes later, I was standing in the reception of Birmingham City University, a security lanyard around my neck, watching the students pouring in and out of an extremely impressive modern building. Part of me looked on enviously at the youth of today who were broadening their knowledge before embarking on their working lives. I reminded myself of what a fool I had been to flunk my education all those years ago.

Professor Wilson soon greeted me with a welcoming smile and a comfortably firm handshake. He immediately put me at ease by insisting that I call him David. It was lunchtime so we agreed to eat in the student restaurant – my treat, the least I could do in return for the Professor giving up his valuable time free of charge. We resisted the urge to delve into the case at once as I explained that I wanted to record our conversation. The background noise from other diners would have adversely affected the quality of that recording and made it more difficult for me to transcribe when I got home.

Lunch was good and very reasonably priced. Always a consideration when you've a tight budget to stick to. Not long afterwards, we were in Professor Wilson's office and ready to roll. During our conversation he made reference to the TV presenter Jill Dando and three other, previously unmentioned cases, so I'll give a bit of background to them now.

Fifty-two-year-old Derrick Bird was a taxi driver who lived in Cumbria. On 2 June 2010, armed with a shotgun and a rifle, he went on a murderous shooting spree. His first victim was his twin brother, David. Bird then slaughtered another eleven entirely innocent people and injured many more before killing himself. The case remains one of the worst multiple murder rampages of our time.

Frank McPhie was a notorious and distinctly unsavoury Glasgow criminal. He had a number of convictions for armed robbery and large-scale drug dealing. In 2000, he was killed on the doorstep of his home by a single shot to the head, fired from a .22 rifle with a telescopic sight (the rifle was later discovered on the eighth floor of a block of flats overlooking McPhie's home). The case has remained stubbornly unsolved for the past eighteen years. In 2014, Police Scotland appealed for information about the crime and insisted the investigation remained 'ongoing'.

Gulistan Subasi was only twenty-six years old when she was shot dead on the doorstep of her mother's home in Hackney, East London, in March 2010. Her killer was a fifteen-year-old boy named Santre Sanchez Gayle, whose interests included girls, football and playing on his Xbox. He was also a self-confessed cannabis dealer, who collected his first criminal conviction for attempted robbery at the age of fourteen. Gayle was sentenced to life imprisonment, with a minimum term of twenty years for what the judge described as 'an efficient, ruthless and calculated execution'. Outside court, Detective Chief Inspector Jackie Sebire commented, 'The frightening thing is his confidence and lack of remorse. Even though he is only fifteen, he knew what he was doing.'

I opened up by explaining to the Professor what I hoped would be the campaigning element to this book, how it might move the case forward and help in the quest for more information to be made public. In particular, I said how much I would like sight of the post-mortem report. Professor Wilson is a vastly experienced media contributor so he understood my desire to campaign for more information. I explained that I would like to know whether Alistair Wilson received any other injuries, if it appeared that he tried to defend himself and whether he had attempted to wrestle the weapon from the gunman.

He had been previously described to me as being 6 foot, 2 inches tall and weighing in at around thirteen-and-a-half stone, a fit and physically able young man. Information about any other possible injuries he received might give us some indicator as to the physical capabilities of the gunman, from which experts like the Professor might be able to reach some authoritative conclusions.

Building on some of what Professor Canter had discussed, I also explained how keen I was to establish the order in which the shots were fired. I also wanted to know what Professor Wilson thought about the shot to the face – two expert opinions must be better than one.

Professor Wilson said: 'Well, the first thing to say is that the idea of attacking the face is something I am very familiar with from my academic research and my work with violent men. Because clearly, when you shoot someone in the face you're destroying the very visible representation of self. You're rubbing out their very being and how they would be seen. And of course, it's significant, isn't it, that when we think of our worst-ever spree killing in Whitehaven and Cumbria, when Derrick Bird shot his brother David, who was his twin, he shoots him first of all in the face, he is literally wiping out a genetic carbon copy of himself, which echoes the fact that he eventually will commit suicide. So, the face is very important in terms of humiliating the victim by the killer.

'But what first interested me, Peter, was not so much the

order of the shots. What first interested me was the doorstep, the fact that this was happening on the doorstep and the doorstep being a liminal space. It's neither one thing nor the other, it's on the threshold of the private but also of the public. I therefore get really interested in to what extent was this a very personalised attack, as opposed to something that was just business. If this was indeed a contract killer, "I am just doing business and it isn't personal, it's impersonal". So, the doorstep, for me, this liminal space, was really what first attracted me to even investigating this story. Because, as you and I will know, there are a very limited number of shootings of this kind, at the doorstep. Obviously, there's Jill Dando; obviously, there's the Glasgow case of Frank McPhie, but there's also the killing of Gulistan Subasi in London. And that's what first attracted my attention: the doorstep. Was it the doorstep because this was something which was domestic, and private, and personalised, and would be solved by thinking about those issues, or was this simply instrumental that it was chosen as the doorstep; this is where we know we can find you at this particular point in time?

'It's always interesting, the phrase "doorstepping" is something that comes from journalism, and if you speak to journalists and you say, "Why are you going to their doorstep?" they say, "Well, we just know they're in, and we've been watching them for a wee while and we now know that we can get access to them." So, I wasn't so much aware of the order of the shootings, and that didn't initially attract my attention, it was just more about the face and the doorstep.'

I then asked, 'If this was not a contract killing in the

classic sense of the word, what do you make of the shot, or shots, to the face?'

The Professor replied, 'The shots to the face, in particular, would imply how personalised this was, and how the killer wanted to express a very deep-seated anger, resentment towards Mr Wilson, and how by shooting him in the face he was able to regain some agency and status over Mr Wilson because of other things that had happened that we are not yet aware of. So, attacking somebody in the face implies something which is very personal and interpersonal about the victim and the perpetrator. There is some research, though, that some contract killers will also have been contracted to attack the face after the person has been killed because the contractor has some personal grievance against the victim. So, there is a complexity there, but initially, all that attracted me about discussing Alistair Wilson's case at all was the fact that it took place on the doorstep.'

'If we park the contract killer to one side and we explore the possibility of somebody with a disturbed mind doing this killing, is there anything that would be an indicator of that to you, apart from the obvious, horrific nature of the crime?' I then asked.

Professor Wilson was clear: 'No, anything is possible in a cold case and an unsolved case. But for me, the disturbed mind, there are a number of things that for me would argue against that hypothesis. The first is that people with disturbed minds who commit this kind of crime are usually well-known and quickly caught. And there is a level of organisation in this particular crime that would also suggest to me that we are not dealing with somebody who is psychotic. Firstly, he seemed to have an element of disguise. The baseball hat pulled over his face implies a knowledge that he should be careful about his appearance. The fact that he was able to escape detection. The fact that he disposed of the weapon. All of those are very conscious pieces of behaviour that one would not expect to see associated with someone who had disordered thinking. Above all, to be able to avoid detection is very difficult if you are psychotic. You give off a lot of local information, both in terms of who you are and what you say about who you are, and also in terms of the clues that you leave behind.'

'Might you confess to someone?' I enquired.

Professor Wilson: 'You would, definitely. There is a real desire by people who have psychosis to confess, but we've got a problem there, in that often people who are psychotic will falsely confess, which is why, as you very well know, the police often keep back details that only the killer will be aware of, so as to rule out those people who want to turn up and say you've been looking for me, I'm the guy wot done it. So, I would tend to see this as much more organised.'

The Professor continued: 'Here's the other thing though that I would say to you. I've parked to one side the idea that this could be a contract killer. I've parked that to one side, but when I first did my research about contract killing, I talked about the doorstep very much as being the site of the master hitman. But then as time has gone on since I published that research, I am increasingly aware of how the doorstep is simply used instrumentally. So, for example, the person that killed Gulistan Subasi, in London, was a sixteen-year-old boy, who was wearing a forensics suit and took a taxi to the house where he was going to kill Subasi, and then took a taxi home after he'd done the killing. And the only reason he was caught was he couldn't resist confessing to his mates because he wanted the status of being the person wot done it. Therefore, gradually, over the period of a few months, information, local intelligence, develops, and he is able to be caught. So, my research in relation to thinking about master hitmen only using the doorstep is becoming much more fluid and nuanced.'

I brought the conversation around to what I described as the 'inescapable envelope': 'I plotted a few murders when I was working undercover and when I purported to be a contract killer, for the life of me I cannot understand why somebody who is engaged to do a professional hit would run such a substantial risk of being caught by the whole envelope scenario. Because we both know that the envelope, were it retained by Alistair or recovered by anybody, would have been a potential treasure trove of forensic evidence and more. If it was a contracted killing, when the man in the hat has asked for Alistair by name, Alistair then appears at the front door, why not go bang, bang, bang, you're dead, job done? Why on earth go through this potentially very compromising rigmarole of having a conversation, handing an envelope over, allowing that envelope to disappear from the front door, and all of that? To me, that's another piece of this jigsaw that just doesn't seem to fit.'

Professor Wilson said, 'I think those are very valid points and I'm not ignoring them. All I would say is, if we think about the boy that killed Gulistan Subasi. His name was Santre Sanchez Gayle, he was paid £200 to do this hit. And with that £200, he bought a fake Gucci hat. Santre Sanchez Gayle goes into very carefully wearing a forensics suit, but is caught a number of times on CCTV, outside the flat where Gulistan Subasi lived. He takes a taxi to the site where he is going to commit the murder, and he takes a taxi back after he's committed the killing. So, you've got this strange mix of behaviours which imply organisation and professionalisation, with disorganisation and amateur street. Sometimes therefore, you and I, because we are criminal justice professionals, we like the answer to be kind of clear-cut, to fit into our way of thinking. And sometimes the answer isn't, because people are people and they behave in rather… well, why on earth would they do that? You end up going, "Well, why on earth would they do that?" And so I'm not, I'm certainly not wedded to the idea, as I was initially, that this is the work of a master hitman, somebody who is very skilled and has come into the area, and commits the hit and then leaves the area. Because my research has developed since I published that study, I am much more aware of the doorstep being used by a variety of people for instrumental reasons. It is simply the place that they know they can get access to the victim at a particular period of time.'

But I still had more to ask about the envelope and we were going to hypothesise about the shell casings: 'The envelope was never seen again so to work on the theory that the gunman retrieved it, I think is sensible. Not only that, but let's work on the theory no shell casings were discovered. That's a pretty cool, calm kind of personality, I would suggest.'

Professor Wilson replied, 'So, you're back to that sense of which I think both of us are struggling to make sense of, whereby you've got these mixtures of behaviours which imply something about the personality of the individual that we're describing. Whereby there's information that would tell you that this is a professional, organised hitman who's done it before. But equally, there's information that would suggest to you that this doesn't make any sense in terms of the character that we would want to paint in relation to a character that we could call a professional hitman. There's a mixture of different stories and narratives going on in relation to his control of the crime scene. But, and again, you know, Peter, let me just push you a wee bit, in terms of the analysis and based on the kind of questions you've been asking me, I find this killer was actually very in control of the crime scene. Because, even if he's having Mrs Wilson coming to the door, and handing over an envelope, which you know, there being a variety of different things going on in a very short space of time, I find this killer very controlling and organised about what's going to take place.'

I responded, 'Of course he's in control, and he's really got it together, because when the potentially compromising envelope is handed over to Alistair, Alistair doesn't run upstairs to Veronica and say, "He's gonna kill me, he's gonna kill me." He goes up there and has a conversation, which clearly doesn't give any indicator as to what lay in store for Alistair.'

Professor Wilson agreed: 'Exactly. So, he is very much in control. That's why if we go back to that second question that you asked me, I do not find evidence here of disordered thinking, I find evidence here of calculation rather than disordered thinking.'

'The gunman gives no indicator whatsoever as to what lay in store for Alistair,' I posed.

'Exactly,' Professor Wilson replied.

This would seem to directly challenge the whole notion that the gunman went to negotiate and not assassinate.

'Isn't that a contradiction?' I asked. 'Does this rule out any element of a threat?'

It should be noted here that Veronica Wilson gave no evidence of her husband relaying any element of a threat to her during their conversation about the envelope. That is not to say the gunman hadn't threatened Alistair, or entered into some kind of negotiation, he may just have chosen not to relay that to Veronica.

Professor Wilson replied, 'All I am doing now is hypothesising. And you would be perfectly entitled to say that doesn't hold up, in terms of other evidence you might have. For me, I think Alistair knew full well what was happening and I think he may, and therefore the bigger conundrum is how much had he told Veronica prior to the doorstep incident? How much was she aware of, prior to the doorstep incident? And therefore, she can be both perfectly, legitimately, saying it's a case of mistaken identity, but nothing about this case says to me mistaken identity. This case screams out, "I'm coming for you," and Alistair knows full well why I am coming for you, is what I felt. Therefore, in a sense, was Alistair Wilson trying... my hypothesis is, Alistair Wilson is trying very hard to be like that swan that's swimming very gracefully above the water but is paddling at a hundred miles an hour beneath the surface. And he's paddling at a hundred miles an hour beneath the surface because he's trying to manage his family and their understanding or non-understanding of what the hell is happening on their doorstep.'

'Which brings me back to a particular train of thought that I've had virtually since I first went to Nairn, and that is, if you find out who Alistair Wilson really is, you are more likely to find out why this happened to him and therefore who was responsible for that. So, not who killed Alistair Wilson, who was Alistair Wilson?' I said.

The Professor responded: 'I've always, as I think I say in the *Glasgow Herald* article [an article the Professor had recently written for the newspaper], I've suggested that the only thing that I know of that takes him out of the banal, the ordinary, the Nairn, is the fact that he's working in a business lending division in HBOS, and that we know that similar business lending divisions in HBOS were giving out loans that they should not be giving out, and that that was all going to unravel in a few short years later. And we now know, because of the Financial Services Authority, how much money was bad debt and what had been happening in relation to that bad debt. And how various bankers working in that division were corrupted in a variety of different ways by a number of people in whose interest it was to make sure that they were given access to facilities in the bank that they should not have been given access to. Does that make sense?'

It did.

Professor Wilson continued, 'Because your question is the right question, it seems to me, who is Alistair Wilson? You know, I'm poor Alistair Wilson, why does the killer want to knock on my door? He wants to knock on my door because I am about to resign from HBOS. There was another Alistair Wilson living two hundred yards away from this Alistair

Wilson, why doesn't he knock on his door? Because he's just a local man who doesn't have those things in his background which transcend the banal, the ordinary, the Nairn.'

University commitments were calling, so our all-too-brief time together was soon to be at an end. We had time to be a little mischievous before we parted company. The man who had written to the newspapers, Professor Wilson and myself, namely the armchair detective Nate, had regularly been sending correspondence, but the professor had recently received a letter from him asking whether there was any likelihood of a TV documentary being made on the crime. Nate had asked for the answer to that question to be conveyed in code via social media: red for 'no', green for 'yes' and grey if discussions about such a documentary were ongoing. Both the Professor and I were involved with ongoing discussions with TV production companies so we posed together for a photograph. We then posted it on our Twitter accounts with the words, 'Under grey skies we got together today to discuss the Alistair Wilson case'.

I thanked the Professor effusively for giving up his time and then left. It had been very courageous of Professor Wilson, Professor Canter and Dr Youngs to offer up their views and opinions to me, when only in possession of the information in the public domain, or what I had given them. One day, maybe they'll be made privy to everything the police know about the crime.

I live in hope.

CHAPTER TWENTY-THREE

A CLUB ON THE SLIDE

It was February 2018. Four long months had passed since I'd given the information to the police regarding Livingston Football Club, which had stated the motive for Alistair Wilson's murder lies within the finances of the club. In October 2017, I'd pondered long and hard about whether I should have disclosed that to them, but in the end, I felt obliged to do so. If the information was credible, and I had no reason to suspect it wasn't, then the police were best placed to investigate it thoroughly. They surely would have access to accountants and other financial experts who could do a properly resourced forensic examination of the club's finances. You'll remember that Police Scotland also told me that they had received cooperation from the Bank of Scotland, which was ongoing. They were therefore much better placed to thoroughly bottom that information out. I've never been a fraud or financial crime investigator. Besides, they may have been made privy to this information before and they may have already investigated or discounted it.

After a four-month gap, I thought it was time I contacted the police for an update – I didn't want to spend a lot of time poring over financial records if this was something they had already done. So, I sent them an email and waited. And waited. I appreciate they're very busy people with other murders and probably other kinds of serious crime to deal with, but even an acknowledgement of some description might have been nice, not to mention courteous. A week or so passed, so I chased them up with a phone call. The promised return call did not materialise either.

Nine days after I sent my email, I got a reply:

> Mr Bleksley
> Whilst I really appreciate your co-operation in supplying this information this is still an ongoing live investigation so I cannot disclose the details of this and several other ongoing lines of inquiry.
> Police Scotland remain committed to this investigation and providing the Wilson family with the support and answers they desperately need.
> As previously mentioned if you have any information that may assist the inquiry team I would encourage you to pass it to us for assessment.
> Kind regards
>
> Stuart Alexander
> Detective Inspector

There we go again, that one-way street the police keep putting in front of me.

The Leveson Inquiry, which reported in 2012 into the culture and ethics of the media, had significant implications for police and media relationships, but it never suggested for a moment that they should not talk to one another: they should just act with propriety. I've never wanted anything back door or otherwise dodgy from the police – I wouldn't dream of it – I just wanted meaningful dialogue.

I now had no option but to pursue this information as best I could.

I started by investigating the history of Livingston FC and its finances. Livingston FC has had quite a chequered history since its humble beginnings in 1943. Back then, the club was started as a works team for the employees of an electronics manufacturing company, Ferranti, and the side was known as Ferranti Amateurs. They played in parks and competed in amateur leagues.

In 1948, the club changed its name to Ferranti Thistle when it became a founder member of the Edinburgh and District Welfare Association. They played against fellow works teams from other local companies and industries.

In 1953, Ferranti Thistle entered senior football level after winning election to the East of Scotland League, where they competed for the next twenty-one years. During that time they picked up some silverware and became members of the Scottish Football Association. They moved to a humble pitch with some spectator facilities – City Park in Edinburgh – in 1969.

Clearly a club on the up, in 1974 they won the right to compete in the Scottish League. If they could fix some off-field issues, they would become the League's thirty-eigth club and compete in the Second Division, only a league below giants of Scottish football, like Celtic and Rangers.

They needed to change the name of the club and find a new stadium. The local authority helped significantly when they offered the use of Meadowbank Stadium. This facility had been built to host the Commonwealth Games of 1970. Don Quarrie of Jamaica, David Hemery of England and Ian Stewart of Scotland had all won gold medals there. It was suitably modern, all-seater and ideal. The Ferranti name had to be dropped because of commercial rules surrounding the naming of clubs, so Meadowbank Thistle Football Club was born.

The club's early years in the League were a bit of a struggle, but fortunes improved when Terry Christie became manager in 1980. They were promoted to the First Division in 1983 and a year later, reached the semi-final of the League Cup. As a part-time club, Meadowbank Thistle were always going to struggle to compete against teams with full-time professional players. In 1993, they were relegated to the Second Division.

Not long afterwards, a local businessman and supporter of the club took a controlling interest, and it's around this date of 1993 that I've chosen as the start point for my financial investigations. Reading reams and reams of financial reports and accounts is not to my mind the most exciting thing one can do with one's life and I'm not going to reproduce everything from the pages I've read, but please bear with me as I try to paint as clear a picture as I possibly can of the club's rather complex finances. I'll keep it brief, focusing on what I believe may be potentially relevant.

On 2 February 1993, 'Verimac (NO.59) Limited' was incorporated as a private limited company. On 1 April that year, the company changed its name to Meadowbank Thistle Football Club Limited.

On 29 April 1993, under the Club's Articles of Association, the share capital was described as 23,600 shares valued at £1 each.

On 16 August 1993, Meadowbank Thistle Football Club Limited allotted a further 76,800 shares in the company. These were valued at £1 each. Six shareholders were allotted a total of 14,400 of the 76,800 shares, with one shareholder, William (Bill) Provan Hunter of Edinburgh, being allotted the remaining 62,400, therefore becoming the overwhelming majority shareholder. In all probability Mr Hunter had paid £1 each for these shares, so in return for an investment of £62,400, he had acquired a controlling stake in the club. He was soon listed in company records as the secretary of the controlling company. His occupation was listed as a building contractor.

On 16 January 1996, the company changed its name from Meadowbank Thistle to Livingston Football Club and moved to Almondvale Stadium, although the company continued to trade under the old Meadowbank Thistle name.

The company accounts for the year ended 30 June 1996 reflect this change. Now, with a long-term lease on a new stadium, the value of the tangible assets had swollen massively from £8,872 to £648,727. However, all was not well. The accountants who prepared the financial audit report commented that 'The company's current liabilities exceeded its current assets by £217,708 and there was a cumulative deficit on the profit and loss account of £199,058'.

Mr Hunter's shareholding now stood at 77,198.

On the pitch, things were looking up. The newly named Livingston FC won the Third Division title in the 1995/96 season.

On 4 March 1997, the company's share capital was increased by 100,000 to 200,000. Often, this is used as a vehicle to raise more cash. If those additional shares issued were valued at £1 each, the company would have received £100,000 of investment.

The accounts for the financial year ended 30 June 1997 made interesting reading. The value of the tangible assets of the club had grown to £1,498,107, but there were eye-watering levels of debt. A new director, Dominic Keane, had come on board. He got a mention early on in the report: 'Mr D W Keane, who was recently appointed a director, has had discussions with the company regarding injections of additional funds and he has prepared a business plan and financial projections covering the next two years'. There was mention of bank lending in these accounts, but unfortunately, I have not been able to find the amount that the Bank of Scotland facilitated for the club around that time, but it must have been significant.

There was a stark warning in the accountants' report, 'Should the financial restructuring not proceed then it is likely that the company would then have to be put into liquidation'.

In December 1997, the company increased its nominal capital once again, this time from £200,000 to £400,000. (Nominal capital is cash raised through the issuing of more shares to those who in effect donate cash to the club.) This was becoming an increasingly familiar tactic and was probably a vehicle through which to raise additional investment.

In April 1998, four directors resigned. One new director was appointed. Then on 30 June 1998, William 'Bill' Hunter resigned as a director. By now, his shareholding was a mere 3,065 shares. I wrote to Mr Hunter, explaining all about my book and requesting an interview. He paid me the courtesy of sending a reply but said he was unable to assist due to standing down from the club some years before Alistair Wilson's murder. The major shareholder in the club was now a company called Quillco 39 Limited of Glasgow. They held 340,000 shares, and operated under the direction of Dominic Keane, who was listed in the club's financial report as having eighteen directorships in various companies, four of which were connected to the running of Livingston Football Club.

In May 1999, the nominal capital in the company was doubled from £400,000 to £800,000. That same month, Livingston FC were crowned Champions of the Second Division. It would appear that success on the pitch was coming at a price.

By the time the company filed its financial statements, on 30 June 2000, one could easily have formed the impression that all was well within the club. In their first season in the First Division, they had finished a very creditable fourth. The financial report had an extremely optimistic tone to it: 'This is the second full year in which the group has operated under the control of the present owners. The results for the year show an encouraging turnaround from the previous year, although wage cost will continue to be monitored closely.'

However, all was not well. Under the heading 'Creditors', the accounts reveal that some £1,100,401 was due to be paid within a year and a further £4,016,748 was to be paid to creditors thereafter. Surely this was a club on financial borrowed time.

Quillco 39 Limited was described as the parent company of what was still trading as Meadowbank Thistle Football Club, although it was of course operating as Livingston FC. Quillco 39 Ltd was owed £2,351,985. This parent company was under the joint control of Dominic Keane and a man who was also to become a director of Livingston Football Club, John McGuinness. McGuinness was one of three new directors appointed to the board of the club on 6 June 2000.

In January 1997, John McGuinness was working as a hospital porter, reputedly earning £150 a week. Times were so hard, he was apparently sleeping on his parents' floor. He must have thought his luck had changed forever when he scooped £10 million on the lottery and immediately went on a spending spree, buying a home, numerous cars, enjoying expensive holidays and marrying his girlfriend, Sandra (the wedding reportedly cost £200,000). With some prudent financial planning, this lavish lifestyle may have been sustainable on £10 million, but instead he was persuaded to invest in Livingston Football Club.

Supporters of Livingston FC might have been forgiven for thinking everything was hunky-dory with their beloved club. In the 2000/01 season they won the Scottish First Division by seven points, thereby securing promotion to what some regarded as the promised land of the Scottish Premier League (SPL). Their progress on the pitch in recent years had been stunning, but the new dawn that was to rise did not herald what many fans had dreamt of.

On 28 July 2001, Livingston FC played their first game in the SPL at their home ground, the Almondvale Stadium. They beat Heart of Midlothian 2–1. What a start! The following week, they were to play Glasgow Rangers at their famous Ibrox Stadium. On the eve of that match, a Floating Charge was created by the club in favour of the Bank of Scotland, which meant the bank now had first call on all and any income of the club and all of its property and assets.

Whatever was happening in the boardroom and the bank had little or no effect over matters on the pitch, for that season Livingston FC finished a highly creditable third in the SPL, only behind Celtic and Rangers.

The financial report for the year to 30 June 2001 opened up with a statement from Dominic Keane, now the chairman, who spoke of memorable matches, glittering on-field success and famous victories over rivals. He justified an operating loss by saying it was due to paying player bonuses for winning promotion to the SPL and increased wages following the signing of a couple of players. Keane described the financial reports for the year as 'satisfactory'. He spoke with pride about a new synthetic pitch which had cost £500,000 and was glowing about the banqueting suite and a nightclub, which now formed part of the club's assets. Keane thanked the Bank of Scotland for supporting these projects.

Deeper within the report, the figures painted a frightening picture. If the previous few pages of this chapter gave the impression of a club on the financial slide (while the team rockets upwards), the figures revealed in the 2001 report, submitted in April 2002, were truly astonishing.

Tangible assets were now valued at £5,005,101. Players'

wages and signing-on fees for the year totalled £1,435,440. Other wages and National Insurance accounted for just over £1 million. Bank loans and overdrafts now amounted to £2,597,716, a six-fold increase on the previous year. The net debt of the club on 30 June 2001 stood at, wait for it: £5,963,963. With figures like this, it is very easy to see how John McGuinness, who had guaranteed some of the bank lending against his own lottery-funded fortune, was heading for a financial crash of monumental proportions.

In June 2002, the company finally changed its name from Meadowbank Thistle Football Club Limited to Livingston Football Club Limited.

The club's financial statements for the year to 30 June 2002 were submitted in May 2003. Keane opened up with a statement that read, 'The year under review was one of the most significant in our group's short history. There was success in footballing terms beyond our expectations and the group expanded its non-match day activities with the completion in June 2002 of our £4.5 million business service centre'.

Planning permission had been submitted for a second office block, together with an eighty-five-bedroom hotel and leisure complex. Plans were also afoot for an extension to the nightclub, in order to meet demand. This extension would cost in the region of £1.5 million. There could be no doubting the ambition of the board. Keane was at pains to emphasise these developments would ensure the long-term stability and viability of the company.

There's an expression for people who look affluent but are actually skint: 'They wear mohair suits with shitty pants on'.

Keane had his crystal ball out: 'a significant turnaround into the group's performance will be realised by the year 2004/05'.

Wages and salaries for the financial year amounted to £3,770,718. Creditors due to be paid within one year were owed £3,609,740. Creditors who could be paid after a year were owed a mind-boggling £9,153,273. Bank loans and overdrafts accounted for £7,433,060 of that figure.

More shares had been issued to Keane and McGuinness's parent company, Quillco 39 Limited, in exchange for capital. McGuinness had made a donation of £250,000 to the company. They say that if you want to make a small fortune from football, start with a big one: John McGuinness is the living proof of that. By now the cracks were so wide, no amount of papering them over was to succeed: the Bank of Scotland was encircling the club.

This calamitous set of accounts was the last to be filed under Dominic Keane's leadership.

At around this time the Bank of Scotland was financially involved with other football clubs in the SPL. May I remind you that the bank had merged with the Halifax in 2001 and was known as HBOS. In early 2004 it was reported by the *Sunday Herald* that HBOS controlled £110 million of the SPL club's £160 million debt. Just days before Livingston FC were forced into administration, an HBOS spokesman told the *Herald*, 'People ask if the bank is getting tough. We will continue to remain supportive of all the clubs. We treat each one as a unique company with a unique situation. We take a totally different approach to each one.'

On 4 February 2004, two employees of a company called

Kroll were appointed administrators of Livingston Football Club Limited, as the Bank of Scotland finally decided enough was enough.

One of the administrators' core functions was to rescue Livingston FC as a going concern. They took over the financial management of the club and drew up a list of all the creditors who were owed money. Top of the list were the Bank of Scotland, who were owed £3,624,945. Then there was HM Customs and Excise and the Inland Revenue, who were owed a total of £495,444. There was a further one hundred or so creditors who were owed a total of £2,229,064.

In a bizarre twist of fate, the club enjoyed its finest hour on the pitch while in administration. On 14 March 2004, Livingston FC played Hibernian in the Scottish League Cup Final at Hampden Park. Livingston FC won 2–0. I wonder if all those creditors celebrated as long and as hard as some of the supporters did – probably not would be my guess.

Keane, McGuinness and two other directors resigned their positions on 18 August 2004. In September, the administrators compiled a progress report. They had entered an agreement with a company called Lionheart Management Limited (LML) in July, which would allow LML to manage the trading of the company until proposals that would satisfy the members and creditors of the previous and failed company were in place. Things were not looking good for the individuals and companies who were owed money. The 'Deficiency to Unsecured Creditors' stood at £2,064,098. Clearly, a lot of people stood to lose considerable sums.

Two months later, Alistair Wilson was dead.

Being owed money can do strange things to people;

people have been killed for just a few quid. While Alistair was no longer working at the Edinburgh offices of the bank when Livingston FC ran up the biggest of its debts, he had worked there in the specialist lending department when the club had previously faced the threat of liquidation. This was prior to his posting to Inverness in 1999. So, did he have any involvement in the club's finances? Did he have any ongoing interest after his posting to Inverness? Could my information that his killing was in some way connected to the club's finances be right?

I do not have any concrete evidence of that. In fact, I have no evidence whatsoever to enable me to point a finger at a living soul. But the more I examined the club's finances, the more I felt that information might have a hint of credibility about it. I thought the bank could help me – HBOS had become part of the Lloyds Banking Group plc by the time I was writing this book. Surely they would like to see justice for their employee? I tracked down the relevant part of the bank and sent them some questions. These questions cut across many aspects of Alistair Wilson's professional life, not only his potential involvement with Livingston FC:

1. When did Alistair start work at the bank? Dates have been bandied around in the media, but I would like pinpoint accuracy, please.
2. Please supply details of his postings and progression within the bank. Once again, there is information that has been widely published by the media, but I'm a stickler for detail. For example, did Alistair work in Edinburgh for a time? Dates, job title and description, please.

3. At the time of his death, Alistair was reportedly working as a 'Business Banking Manager' in the bank's offices in Inverness. Please confirm this. What were his roles and responsibilities within this title? Please provide as much detail as possible. For example, did Alistair have the authority to convert an overdraft into a loan? Did Alistair attend business functions at hotels and similar venues, in an attempt to persuade businesses to bring their custom to the Bank of Scotland? Any other facts detailing what Alistair's role entailed would be appreciated.

4. In his role as a Business Banking Manager, would Alistair have been permitted to refund bank charges to businesses if he deemed it appropriate?

5. Did Alistair, his immediate colleagues or his bosses during any of his postings at the Bank of Scotland ever have dealings with the finances of the following professional football clubs: Rangers, Hearts, Aberdeen, Livingston, Dundee United or Dunfermline? If so, please supply whatever details you can.

6. What was Alistair's salary and bonus package at the time of his death? If the bank cannot disclose this, may I please be furnished with a list of pay scales for those working within the Business Banking Sector of the bank at the time of Alistair's murder. These pay scales would surely have been in the public domain when positions were advertised publicly.

7. Did Alistair have a mortgage or other secured loan with the bank that related to his home, 10 Crescent Road, Nairn?

8. In November 2005, Alistair's widow Veronica inherited £4,940.04, which were bonuses due to Alistair from

the Bank of Scotland. Over what period of time had Alistair accrued these bonuses? What duties had Alistair performed to become eligible for these bonuses?

9. It has been widely reported that at the time of his death, Alistair was working his notice period at the bank. Is this true? If so, when did Alistair hand his notice in to the bank? When was he due to work his last day for the bank?

10. Was Alistair ever subject to any discipline procedures whilst working for the bank? If so, please supply whatever details you can.

11. It was widely reported in the local media that Alistair, his wife Veronica and her brother Iain were running a bed-and-breakfast and restaurant business at their home, Lothian House, 10 Crescent Road, Nairn, in December 2002. This was while Alistair was also working for the bank. Was the bank aware of this? Was this permitted by the bank? Did it not create a potential conflict of interest for a bank employee to be also running a business?

The bank's response was an all-too-familiar one:

Hi Peter,

Just coming back to you on your query.
     I'm afraid that because of colleague confidentiality we do not have any information to share on this request.

I was livid. I guess I shouldn't have been. The refusal of the police to answer my questions should have prepared me for this strikingly similar response from the bank. However, I was not taking this particular no for an answer.

The nightmare that was Livingston Football Club did not end for Dominic Keane and John McGuinness with the appointment of administrators. In August 2009, Keane went on trial in Edinburgh, charged with fraud. The allegation against him was that he presented documents to John McGuinness which bore forged signatures. This episode surrounded efforts to secure more funding from the bank for the development of the club's Almondvale Stadium in 2001. McGuinness gave evidence during which he told the court that he had lost between £3 and £4 million during his involvement with the club and that he had nothing left from his £10 million lottery win. Keane told the court how his involvement with Livingston FC had caused him to lose his home and become bankrupt. He was hugely relieved when a jury returned a 'not guilty' verdict after only forty-five minutes of deliberation.

As Keane left the court, he ruled out any future involvement with football and said, 'I'm going to enjoy the rest of my life.'

In January 2018 I wrote to him. I had plenty of questions that I wanted to put to him. If there was anybody who might know about Alistair Wilson's possible involvement with the club's finances, it must surely be Mr Keane. I'm still waiting for a reply.

CHAPTER TWENTY-FOUR

THE NORTHERN BLIGHTS

I don't regard myself as famous, because frankly, I'm not. I have about 10,000 followers on Twitter and occasionally I'm recognised in the street. Generally speaking, it's by fans of *Hunted*, who want a selfie and a natter about the show. These people are always lovely and I make sure that I give them my time. There are other benefits to having a minor public profile. Sometimes I'm asked to go into schools to speak to the pupils, present prizes or give careers advice, when I generally sell the idea of joining the police or becoming a writer to the youngsters.

I've recently been asked to get involved with the Kiyan Prince Foundation (KPF). Kiyan was a hugely talented footballer who was on the books of my beloved Queens Park Rangers FC when he was stabbed to death in 2006. He was only fifteen years old. Kiyan's dad Mark, who was a world-class professional boxer, has since dedicated his life to persuading youngsters to lay down their weapons and thereby stop killing each other. Mark asked me to come on board and of course I jumped at the chance. Quite how an ageing, overweight, grey and balding uncool bloke like me is going to engage with teenagers, we've yet to find out, although I do have teenagers of my own. I'm really going to give this a go. Hopefully, my TV profile will help. I can give first-hand experience of what it's like to be stabbed in the neck, I've stared down the barrel of a gun a few times and spent a lot of time with grieving parents, siblings and friends. If I can convince just one young person that carrying a weapon is a recipe for disaster then that will be an achievement.

I've also been invited to become an ambassador for a charity that does some amazing work with child victims of crime. Once we've nailed what the charity's expectations are of me, I'm sure we'll progress with that as well.

In the Highlands I'm known to quite a few people because of my research into Alistair Wilson's murder. Many of these people have repeatedly asked me to look at another local and mystifying unsolved case that happened back in 1976. These concerned folk have often tried to convince me to write a book about this crime, but there are a number of unsolved murders or unexplained deaths that I'm currently considering, including some where the families have asked me to take on their case. I'm well aware of the significant impact that unsolved murder and unresolved death cases have, not only on families and friends, but on local communities, who still hope for justice decades after the crime has been committed, so I'll always do whatever I can to highlight these crimes.

Renee MacRae's life was not exactly straightforward. She was married to Gordon MacRae, although they lived separately. Renee had two sons, Gordon who was aged nine and Andrew who was three. Some years earlier, around 1971, she had begun an affair with a man called Bill McDowell, who was married with two kids. McDowell worked for Renee's husband Gordon as an accountant and company secretary. This clandestine affair was a well-kept secret. It was reported at the time that McDowell was, in fact, the father of Renee's three-year-old son Andrew.

On Friday, 12 November 1976, Renee left her home in Inverness, driving her BMW with both her sons with her. She dropped off her nine-year-old son Gordon at the home of her estranged husband, before eventually venturing onto the A9, heading south. Sometime later, her BMW was discovered ablaze in a layby, south of Inverness. Renee and Andrew were missing; they have never been discovered, alive or dead.

The Northern Constabulary carried out an inquiry which unearthed a web of lies and deceit, but never brought anyone to trial for the murders of Renee and Andrew. Over the years, the case has stubbornly refused to go away. In 2004, at great expense, police excavated Dalmagarry Quarry, near Tomatin, without success. All that was found were two crisp packets and some rabbit bones. There have long been rumours that Renee and Andrew were buried beneath the A9 and while high-tech surveying equipment did reveal an 'anomaly' under a section of that road, bodies were never discovered.

In 2006, the Northern Constabulary claimed it had 'closed the evidential gap' and submitted a report to the Crown Office. The Crown Office later reported that there was 'insufficient evidence for criminal proceedings against any person at this time'.

In 2016, on the fortieth anniversary of Renee and Andrew's disappearance, the family told how they were 'collectively heartbroken' and Police Scotland's Major Investigations Team spoke of their determination to find answers. Detective Superintendent Jim Smith said, 'The passage of time is no barrier and we continue to urge anyone who may have information that could assist the investigation to come forward.' If you are that person and you'd rather speak to me, my contact details are on the last page of this book.

I was recently contacted by the family of a young man who died in circumstances that are far from clear. It is another case where the Northern Constabulary fell way short of the standards the public should expect from them.

In case you're thinking one of the main purposes of this book is to give the police a literary bashing to which they have no opportunity to reply, let me point out that it's not. I know from harsh experience how challenging policing can be, but I make no apology for highlighting police failings. When you are paid out of the public purse to serve the public, the standards you abide by must be of the absolute highest, without compromise. Service must come before self, no matter what the circumstances, always. The majority of police officers abide by that ethos day in, day out, often in the face of provocation, threats and all too frequently, violence. However, some do not. The failings, neglect, conspiracies and law breaking of those officers must be exposed and they must be rooted out. They must be jailed, if necessary. Police officers are entrusted with the highest power, the ability to deprive someone of their liberty. In return, they must be above and beyond reproach.

Kevin McLeod was a twenty-four-year-old much-loved young man. Known as a highly efficient, tidy and conscientious electrician, he lived in the Highland town of Wick, approximately one hundred miles north of Nairn. He was engaged to be married to Emma and was very proud of his Ford Sierra Cosworth car.

Kevin had recently taken possession of a council house, which was soon to become his marital home. On Friday, 7 February 1997, he put in a full day's work. Afterwards, he joined his mum and his aunt, who were busy cleaning the new house, getting it spick and span for moving-in day. That evening, he was persuaded by a friend to go for a drink and a game of pool. His friend picked him up at about 10 p.m. The full story of what happened in the next few hours has never been definitively told, but when Kevin had not returned home by 3 a.m., those near and dear to him became alarmed.

The following day, anxious family members spoke to local people, they made many phone calls and searched 'every nook and cranny'. These included cliffs, sheds, the harbour and more. At 5.25 p.m. on Saturday, 8 February, Kevin was reported missing to the police.

The next day, the police were apparently told that somebody had seen Kevin kneeling down in the foetal position near a lamp post in the early hours of the Saturday morning. The police called a local diver rather than a fully-fledged police diving team and at around 11 a.m. on the Sunday, this diver found Kevin's body in the harbour.

It has been alleged to me that a local PC informed the

family there were 'no suspicious circumstances' surrounding Kevin's death, even though his body was still in the water. A relative posed the question to me, 'How could he say that?' Kevin's body was transported to Inverness for a post-mortem.

The post-mortem revealed that he had suffered severe abdominal injuries before entering the harbour. These injuries were such that if left untreated, they could have proved fatal. They could have been consistent with Kevin receiving 'a kicking' some time before he entered the water. The pathologist informed the Procurator Fiscal of this.

Despite this, Detective Sergeant Richard Martin of the Northern Constabulary (now deceased) informed the family that their loved one's death was due to a 'tragic accident'. DS Martin continued, 'Kevin was walking home at speed and fell into an ornamental street board. He got up to relieve himself and fell into the harbour.' But Kevin's family did not accept that explanation; they had received word that there had been an 'altercation' on the waterfront, during which he had been assaulted. What was not known to the family at this stage was that the Procurator Fiscal had instructed DS Martin to treat Kevin's death as if it were a murder and conduct a suitably resourced major inquiry. DS Martin did not do this, which of course begs the question, 'Why not?' Some ten years later, the Procurator Fiscal was asked to recall the exact words he used in the instruction to DS Martin and he remembered using the expression, 'the full works'. Inexplicably, and unforgivably, Kevin's clothing, which could have provided vital forensic evidence, was destroyed by the police.

Instead of possible arrests, charges and a criminal trial, in 1998 a Fatal Accident Inquiry was held. The family wanted to call particular witnesses that they had identified but they were denied the opportunity by the Crown. The Sherriff presiding gave a concluding speech, during which he said, 'Prior to death the Deceased sustained severe abdominal injuries, as described in detail... These injuries were sustained a relatively short time, probably less than one hour, prior to his immersion in the water of the harbour. Their severity was such that if untreated, they would themselves inevitably have proved fatal and even if prompt surgical intervention had been available, survival would have been uncertain. The causation of these injuries has not been established. The central issue in the inquiry was whether the Deceased's abdominal injuries resulted from an assault or an unobserved accidental fall. The evidence has proved insufficient to enable me to answer that question one way or the other. It has not been established that the Deceased's very serious abdominal injuries resulted from his having been assaulted, but that remains a possibility.'

An open verdict was returned.

The family made a number of complaints to the police about their mishandling of the investigation into Kevin's death. Despite various inquiries into different aspects of police behaviour, they felt they just weren't getting to the truth, the whole truth and nothing but the truth. They took their concerns to 10 Downing Street and still they failed to get the answers they craved.

In 2002, a witness came forward and alleged that on the night he died, Kevin had been assaulted by a police officer, who had kicked him in the stomach and solar plexus. This witness has since died. Still, the family campaigned relentlessly. At times they felt the entire establishment was conspiring to frustrate their quest to establish the truth about exactly what happened.

In 2003, a retired and vastly experienced former murder squad detective contacted the family, offering to help. His efforts to interview officers involved in the case were unsuccessful. He was moved to say, 'This is the first time in the number of cases I have examined since I left the force that the obstruction I've encountered has been so blatant. This case stinks.'

Professor Ed Friedlander, a leading pathologist from the US, gave his opinion, 'The pathology is perfect for homicide.'

The years rolled by, the obfuscation continued, but still the family somehow found the strength to continue pursuing the truth.

In December 2017, more than twenty years after Kevin's death, Police Scotland met with Kevin's parents and issued a press release:

Since this tragic incident, numerous investigations have substantiated the family's belief that there were serious failings on the part of Northern Constabulary in both the initial and subsequent handling of this case. There is no doubt that basic policing procedures were never carried out and the opportunity to gather vital evidence was missed.

Legacy policing services undoubtedly failed this family and I am further disappointed that their complaints were treated in a dismissive manner in the years which followed Kevin's death. During a recent comprehensive reassessment of this case Police

Scotland has come to the conclusion that, because of the initial police investigation failures and based upon the evidence now available, we are unable to present any evidence which would clearly indicate the circumstances surrounding the cause of Kevin's death, either criminally or accidentally.

Kevin's death remains as unexplained, as directed by the Crown Office and Procurator Fiscal Service (COPFS). Police Scotland is fully committed to investigating any new evidence which may come to light. I fully understand that such a conclusion must be difficult for Kevin's family to accept and on behalf of the policing service I regret the pain and anguish that this has caused them over such a long period of time. I hope that this unreserved apology may go some way to bring some form of closure to Kevin's family and once again on behalf of Police Scotland I apologise unreservedly for the past failings of the police services in Scotland.

Of course, the last line is complete nonsense. How dare the police speak of 'closure' when the family still seek answers to so many of their questions. I've spent some time speaking to the family and I've put them in touch with a television production company. I'd love to be a part of a thorough investigation which could become a documentary. I'd very much like to cut a swathe through the fog of obstruction and wrongdoing that's plagued this case for over two decades. Unfortunately, I'm not a TV decision maker, so in that regard it's out of my hands, but I'm doing all I can. While some witnesses have died, many remain alive and well – in fact, a new witness came forward only recently. The truth can be found. Watch this space…

CHAPTER TWENTY-FIVE

SCARPERED

April 2018. The deadline for delivering the manuscript of this book to my publisher was rapidly approaching.

I rang Tom Randall. We'd kept in touch over the years and in the nine years since we'd last visited Nairn together, he'd gone on to forge a very distinguished career in TV. He'd directed a number of very well received documentaries and formed his own bespoke production company, Wiretap Productions. His interest in Alistair Wilson's murder remained strong and I often brought him up to speed with my progress. He accepted my invitation to join me on what would be my last trip to Nairn before submitting my manuscript: he'd bring his cameras with him, we'd shoot anything of interest and possibly make a pitch on our return to London. I warned that in order to protect their identities, a number of my sources might not wish to meet him and I could not guarantee any TV gold. Nonetheless, he agreed to keep me company and said this trip would be, 'One hundred per cent your gig'.

The main purpose of this trip would be to try and get in front of Shaun Douglas – I had plenty of questions that I wanted to put to him. I didn't have any evidence to suggest that he was involved in Alistair's murder, but I knew the police were keen to interview him (they had questioned both Keith and Craig Douglas about Shaun). There was also the issue of the envelope with Craig's first name 'Paul' being on it, but that might be a completely unrelated coincidence. None of this forms any kind of case against Shaun Douglas whatsoever, but I really wanted to give him the opportunity to say his bit. By then I had spoken to his dad, his brother Craig and I'd had a telephone conversation with his sister. I'd asked them all to persuade Shaun to call me; they all had my number. I knew for a fact that his father Keith had passed my number on, yet he still refused to call – that is, of course, his right.

Tom drove his car over to my house early on a Monday morning. It was the school holidays so my darling wife had a day off work and was going to give us a lift to the airport. All those years earlier, in 2009, Tom had bought my boys a classic book (a Greek fable, although the title escapes me now), so I made sure they got their teenage backsides out of bed to say hello and goodbye to him.

As is so often the case, one of my sources had been busy. A week or so before this trip, I had informed him that Shaun Douglas had apparently left his dad's house and that his whereabouts were unknown. Could my source find Shaun in Nairn? The source rang me a couple of days later and told me that Shaun had apparently been staying in town with a man called Mike, near to his dad's house. My source was making inquiries to try and identify an address for Mike. I didn't have long to wait before my source rang me again, this time with an address. Following this, I did some inquiries of my own and confirmed that Mike's surname was linked to the address given to me by my source.

Please let Shaun be staying there when I get to Nairn, I thought.

I looked out over snow-capped mountains as our delayed flight approached Inverness Airport. Soon afterwards, at the car hire desk, the inquisitive clerk asked me what the purpose of my trip was and I told her. She said, 'Oh, there's a detective writing a book on that case.' 'Yes, that's me,' I responded. I was immediately attributed minor celebrity status by this engaging young woman, who was quick to offer her thoughts on the crime. Despite the queue behind us I felt obliged to take a little bit of time to point out to her that I thought her theory was wrong and my reasons why. I declined her offer to upgrade my car at considerable expense and left her suitably informed of my opinion.

Tom now has a family of his own, including a boy of four called Louis, the same age as Alistair Wilson's eldest son when his father was murdered. I detected a flicker of emotion in Tom's voice as I reminded him of that fact.

While held at traffic lights in town, Tom was convinced he saw Veronica Wilson walking past us. She had apparently looked into our car and would doubtless have recognised me. I had my eyes on the traffic ahead and hadn't seen her. This reminded me of Shaun Douglas's likely innocence. Living as close as he did to Veronica, there had to be high probability that in a small town such as Nairn they would probably have passed one another in the street. Even though everyone who knew Shaun had described him to me as a night owl, who only came out during the hours of darkness, he must have surfaced sometimes during the day. Surely Veronica would recognise him were they ever to pass in the street and the chance of that happening had to be a lot higher than if they lived in a major city. Having said that, if Veronica's sighting of the gunman had been clear then once again I pondered why an e-fit or an artist's impression hadn't been produced (I know I've mentioned it before, but this is a nagging question that will not leave me). Even a sketch showing the build, cap and other clothing of the gunman could have been helpful to the public and should definitely have been produced.

I'd adopted a completely different attitude towards this trip. Because I was keen to speak to Shaun Douglas, who seemed reluctant to speak to me, we were travelling under the radar. I steered clear of social media and the press and hoped we would arrive largely unannounced. There was no way that Shaun or his associates would know we were in town. Tom and I booked into The Braeval Hotel and made our way to our rooms, all of which had been recently decorated and were looking in fine form.

At around 7.30 p.m. Tom and I took the short walk from our hotel, past Veronica's front door and on to the road where Mike lived – as a matter of courtesy, I wasn't going to knock on the door any later. I wondered if the gunman had given much thought to the timing of his appearance at Alistair's front door. If he'd left it much later, say eight or nine o'clock, then perhaps Veronica or Alistair might not have answered.

I rang the front doorbell. Tom was keeping eyeball on the back in case anybody decided to leg it. Not that there was much we could have done because we're not the cops. A man in his forties, casually dressed and wearing a beanie hat, answered the front door. I identified myself to him and he confirmed that he was the Mike I'd been looking for. During the course of our conversation, Mike admitted that he and Shaun had been friends since the late 1980s and that this friendship stemmed from their mutual interests in heavy metal music, computer games and movies. I told him that I was looking for Shaun. Mike then told me that he thought Shaun would be at his dad's house. I told him that I'd heard Shaun had been staying with him, but Mike was quick to deny that his friend had ever lived with him.

I brought the conversation around to Alistair Wilson's murder, asking if Shaun had ever discussed the case with Mike: 'He brought it up now and again. He thought it strange as well.'

I asked, 'What did Shaun talk about when he discussed the case?' I wanted to know.

Mike sternly replied, 'He thought he would get stitched up by the police for it, he always had a thing about that.'

I asked why Shaun would be fearful of this and Mike responded, 'It might be as a result of his upbringing, he went to boarding school.'

I asked when Shaun last expressed those fears to Mike.

'Last year,' he said.

It seemed Shaun also expressed this fear of being stitched up some years earlier.

One thing that should go some way towards allaying Shaun's fears of being stitched up is the description of the gunman given to police by Veronica Wilson. She described him as being between 5 foot, 4 inches and 5 foot, 8 inches tall and stocky. Shaun has been described to me as being 5 foot, 10 inches or thereabouts and weighing in at about thirteen stone. There is, however, a step at the very front of Veronica's house that is about four inches tall. This means that someone standing inside the house would be in a position some inches higher than a person standing immediately outside the house on the short concrete pathway. This of course could skew someone's perception of how tall a caller at the front door might be. I have often wondered whether the officer who took Veronica's original statement, which included the description, was aware of this step and factored it into her recollections. Height is so often a very difficult thing for witnesses to accurately recall. Many people do not accurately know their own height and are therefore not very good at estimating the height of others. Maybe Shaun is right to be fearful.

Mike told me that he and Shaun could go months without seeing each other, but I left my contact details and asked him to convince his friend to call me the next time he saw him. Mike said that Shaun had spoken about travelling to Europe. We shook hands and parted.

I immediately got on the phone to Shaun's dad, Keith. He reiterated what he had told me when we spoke a few weeks earlier, that he'd given Shaun an ultimatum, which he repeated to me: 'I'm gonna tell you, if they [the police] keep coming up here and knocking on my door, the locks will be changed and you won't be able to get back in here. So, get yourself sorted out, ring them up and answer the questions.' Keith told me that he had not seen or heard from his son since he made things plainly clear, three weeks earlier. I asked if he knew where he might be: 'I've no idea where he is… he's scarpered altogether.'

Tom and I returned to the hotel. I was bitterly disappointed that I hadn't found Shaun; I had desperately wanted to give him the opportunity to give me his opinions on the fear of being fitted up and more. My last chance to speak to him before delivering my manuscript was gone and I was gutted.

I think you, the public, have a right to know how the police investigation into Alistair Wilson's murder is progressing. There remains huge public interest in this case, not only among the people of Nairn, but way beyond that. In nearly fourteen years the police have never made an arrest in connection with this crime. They have gone on public record saying that they have never established a motive for Alistair's killing.

The day before I wrote this passage, I was speaking at a literary lunch in Hull. Towards the end of my speech I informed the audience that I was writing a book on this case and I gave them a taster of what was to come. As I signed books afterwards a number of people told me that they remembered the case and were keen to hear more. Shaun Douglas has a right to privacy, of course he has. He also has the right to walk freely down the road without fear of being accused of being a murderer. I for one am not accusing him of killing Alistair Wilson, but there are a number of questions the police want to put to him, as do I. And you, the great British public, have the right to be informed about that. I've offered Shaun plenty of opportunities to be quoted within these pages. Unfortunately, he has refused to get in touch. If he does make contact with me and chooses to answer my questions, I can assure him that the next edition of this book will be fully updated with his answers.

I sat in my hotel room and cursed to myself. But I thought that I might as well publicise the fact that I was now in town so I posted across social media that I was in Nairn. I contacted a number of sources and told them the same. Then I went to Tom's room for a moan. He tried to convince me that we should go for a drink. I wasn't feeling particularly sociable. Tom lifted my mood considerably by saying how good it was that the pair of us were working together again, if only for a few days. He was right; I decided I'd go for that drink, nothing would be achieved by feeling sorry for myself. We went downstairs to the bar, which was deserted. Sod that! We walked the short distance to The Havelock. That wasn't much busier, but the delightful barmaid explained that Monday nights were always quiet because it was dominoes night and the only places that would be a bit lively would be the bars where the domino league games were being played. She kindly looked up the fixtures for us and told us where the games were on. Four bars were hosting dominoes that night. She described them all and firmly pointed out the one we should avoid because it was 'rough'. That was it, our choice was made.

A warm and engaging barman welcomed us to the 'rough' bar. Now, my wife might not choose it as a favoured place to go for a glass of wine – in fact, I didn't see a bottle of wine in there, but believe you me, this bar looked like a day nursery compared to some of the pubs and clubs I've been in over the years. Tom and I perched at the bar and ordered a drink. I made no secret of why I was in town and the barman soon offered a theory that I'd never heard before: he told me that Alistair, Veronica and the boys had been relocated to Nairn because they were living in the witness protection programme. I immediately added that opinion to the bizarre and bonkers category. The barman then introduced me to a truly delicious whisky I hadn't savoured before, a twelve-year-old Aberlour. Do try!

Tom and I enjoyed a couple of drinks and discussed other potential projects that we might be able to work on together in the future. My disappointment was beginning to fade. After all, there wasn't much I could do about Shaun Douglas's disappearing trick...

CHAPTER TWENTY-SIX

THE INSIDE TRACK

On a previous trip to Nairn I had spoken briefly on the phone to the man who worked most closely with Alistair Wilson at the Bank of Scotland in the time leading up to his murder. The trouble was this man had been in a hurry to get to work; his schedule and his home life were clearly placing huge demands on his time and he could only talk for a few snatched minutes, certainly not enough time for me to get a thorough picture of Alistair the banker and Alistair the man. A number of calls and texts failed to nail down a date, time and location when we could meet face to face. I was delighted when eventually we agreed to talk during my final trip.

At his request I have given this man a pseudonym – I'm going to call him Callum.

I began by asking him about Alistair Wilson and his family. Callum explained that he had met Veronica about seven or eight times and that her marriage to Alistair appeared, 'Pretty good, pretty solid'. He went on, 'Veronica was a bit older than Alistair and she wore the trousers. Al was a proud dad. All our kids were young so we didn't have a lot of funny stories to share.' I asked if he ever saw Alistair smile: 'Yes, plenty of times.'

Callum described Alistair as having 'an awkward sense of humour, an awkward character. We went to plenty of bank corporate functions. He was an old guy for his age, pretty serious and very career-minded. He was not one for banter, that wasn't his environment. It was difficult for him to get involved in those kinds of conversations, it wasn't his thing. Others who were involved in banter would be uncomfortable with Al being involved in those conversations. At work functions he wasn't backwards with coming forwards.'

Callum was extremely talkative. I asked a few questions as we went along but generally, he offered up his thoughts freely without the need for me to prompt. He continued: 'Al came into the bank as a graduate, so he leapt up a few levels, four levels above people who came into the bank from school. There was a story from his time at the bank in Fort William, where he would say to the boss as he went for lunch, "Is there anything you needed done?" Not many would do that. He was a career guy. If there was a boss in proximity, he would put his best foot forward. In other conversations he could flounder, be a bit awkward, not having whatever it would be to carry it off. He was never the life and soul. He'd have a drink and let his hair down on occasion. In banking, you need to be adaptable depending on the circumstances. He was young when he passed away so he may have developed as he got older. He was better in some circumstances than others.'

I asked Callum to give me his own career history with the bank and he explained that he joined straight from school in 1986. He had various postings before arriving at Inverness in 1999: 'Alistair was already there. His [role] was a manager's assistant, an analyst behind a senior manager, number crunching. He wouldn't lead the relationship with a corporate or commercial business, his role was to take the accounts, crunch them, analyse them and complete a report and feed that to a senior manager. It was a good springboard to taking on a portfolio role, where you had more autonomy. He would have been meeting clients occasionally without the boss being there, but that would be a holding role where he fed the information back to the boss. Al did this between 1999 and 2001. In 2001, there was a re-jig in the bank and from 2001 to 2002, he was in commercial banking, looking after a small team of phone-based, lower-level business managers. That didn't last too long.'

Callum said there was then another shake-up at the bank, which led to Alistair going into a business development manager (BDM) role early in 2002. He went on to explain what that role entailed: 'I joined as a BDM, or "hunter", in August 2002. Me and Al were both hunters, responsible for getting new business into the bank. A business relationship manager would then manage that ongoing relationship. They were known as "farmers". The roles were alternatively known as "catchers" and "tossers" – I'll let you work out who gave us those names. So, the hunter wins the business, writes a paper to our credit colleagues, who would hopefully approve it or approve it with some conditions. Then as soon as the money was drawn down or approved, the farmer would take over. As soon as possible you'd move on to the next one.

'Me and Al were both hunters and we worked alongside each other. I was four or five years older than Al and we both landed in that role from different backgrounds. We sized each other up a little bit and we worked as a team. I wouldn't say we were Toshack and Keegan [Liverpool FC legends] cos we weren't that good, but Al, with his accountancy background, knew all about balance sheets, financial analysis, all that kind of stuff. He didn't have a whole lot of contacts. Those he did have, he'd probably ridden side-saddle behind his previous manager. Maybe he didn't know a whole lot of people in Inverness… I came more from a mortgage, sales and business development background. I brought lots of contacts and a more traditional sales approach. We actually gelled well as a team.'

Alistair and Callum were responsible for covering all of the Highlands and Islands, an area bigger than the size of Belgium. Consequently, there was quite a lot of driving involved. On this, Callum commented, 'If you're gonna have two guys working there, you've got to be quite smart. If Al's going up to Thurso, two-and-a-half hours north, that's a five-hour round trip, so we did share work. We worked collegiately with the files, although we had our own individual targets. We did accept when one of us was better placed to deal with a file.'

I asked if there was ever any cold calling of businesses in an effort to drum up work: 'It rarely came to that. We'd get some business from the farmers… the guy at Orkney was pretty good. We had a lot of professional contacts, accountants, solicitors, brokers, there was always good stuff coming in.

There were some phone-based initiatives, a bank centre in Chester would pick off details from Companies House and cold call them, but I don't remember us having any great need to cold call businesses. We had to suss out quickly which ones would be goers and which ones wouldn't be.'

I wanted Callum to explain what sort of businesses he and Alistair dealt with: 'Our main target was to be borrowing over £100,000. That's quite a broad spectrum in the Highlands and Islands. There were lots of leisure businesses, hotels, guest houses, bed-and-breakfasts of all shapes and sizes. Quite a lot of people would be relocating to the Highlands from further south. They've seen the region on TV or holidayed here, fallen in love with it and followed the dream. Sometimes they last two winters, realise they miss home, it's quieter than they thought in the winter period and that business would be back on the market to be sold to another person from down south. There'd be property deals, guys with plots of land who might look to build four houses, bigger developers, house builders. In those days every house that was built would sell and the market was only going to go one way. Any trading entity really, not a lot was off-limits.'

I asked if there was an upper limit of lending beyond which they would have to refer the file to a more senior manager: 'Probably something like £5 million. If we had a file that big, you'd need at least a co-pilot along with you.'

'Was it a demanding role?' I enquired.

Without hesitation Callum replied, 'It was pretty full on, it certainly wasn't a nine-to-five job – it wasn't a job for everybody. You were putting yourself out there, asking for business. That's not for every banker to do. With Al being an ex-accountant, he was out of his comfort zone a little bit. Potential clients could play you by getting an offer from another bank. Every deal was a bit of a courtship. Some people would come to you in desperation and you'd think, was this a deal I can get through the credit team? There could be a courtship and you could be left at the altar.'

I asked Callum about the credit team, the bank employees who would have the final sign-off on any lending that he and Alistair were trying to obtain for their new customers: 'Me and Al were young and hungry and looking to get bonuses. The credit team probably put the brakes on people like us, or just calmed us down a little bit when we were reaching a bit too much. Every business we did was new to the bank and had to go through a credit process. However, if the hunter signed it off and the farmer signed it off, it could happen without having to go back to credit again.'

Callum gave me his views on the culture of the bank during the time he and Alistair worked together as a team: 'The culture of banking in the Highlands was probably different from the Central Belt and certainly London. Here, there was money to be made. Me and Al had a basic salary in the mid-twenty thousands. We weren't paying into pensions, they were non-contributory, and if you stayed at the bank, you were going to get two-thirds of your salary as a pension. We had bank cars, Mondeos, we didn't pay anything for that. There were lots of fringe benefits, a save-as-you-earn scheme where you paid in, say, £40 a month that would go to buy some bank shares. In five years that would roll out. Fifty pounds a month could give you £2,000–£3,000-a-year payout.

'The main bit was that you could earn up to 50 per cent of

your basic as a bonus. It had to be earned across so many deals a year. You couldn't land on two cases for £6 million in the first month and then sit back with a cigar, you needed a certain amount of profit for the bank each year over a certain number of deals. If you got your big ones early on, you'd pick up another couple of smaller ones to tick that box. It was a decent gig. It was enough money to keep the wives happy, bring up a couple of kids and have a decent lifestyle in the Highlands rather than flogging yourself to death in the big city.'

I wanted to know if Callum knew exactly what Alistair's basic salary was: 'I was on £26,000 basic, Al was on £24–£26,000. With bonuses, that could get up to £40,000.'

'Did the bank put profits before principles?' I asked.

Here, Callum used an interesting metaphor: 'At no point did we think that six years later, the banks would be teetering and needing bailouts. For myself and Alistair, our job was like being a paramedic. It was our job to turn up when a case was urgent. It was our job to get it [the client's business] to the hospital still alive. Sometimes businesses were on the cusp, would they go this way or that way? Our job was to get it strong enough to get through the door, signed off by the farmer, and thank you, we were on to the next one. You were probably dealing with twelve, fourteen cases at a time. If you were dealing with a business, you were thinking, right, get this one over the line... Could that business actually work? Get that one drawn down, get the hotel bought. After that, I'd never have to give an arse again. Rewards drive behaviours. If you're rewarding guys with up to 50 per cent of their basic, then yeah, rewards drive behaviours.'

I found that answer particularly interesting. Here was

an admission that Callum and Alistair were dealing with businesses sometimes in trouble. Those were exactly the sort of scenarios that prompted corrupt behaviour, although there is no suggestion that Callum or Alistair behaved with impropriety.

Callum explained that bonuses were earned during the calendar year, from January to December. I pointed out that Alistair only earned some £4,000 in bonuses in 2004; I knew this because the amount had been made public many years earlier. Alistair was shot near the end of November so he was clearly some considerable way short of the £12,000 or £13,000 he might have accrued in a successful year.

Callum replied: 'Al didn't have as good a year as he wanted in 2004. Myself and Al both had deals up in Orkney that year. Mine came off, it was a good deal. Alistair invested a lot of time that year working with a building company, house building in Orkney. He felt he'd been let down by credit, who didn't approve it. That's how it was in those days. If that Orkney deal had gone through, he would have earned his full bonus. As a bonus, four grand was quite a way short of what you'd be looking for. That was what turned Al's mind to looking for other things.'

We discussed Alistair's move to the BRE Group. I asked Callum what he knew of that: 'I think the basic was going to be £40,000. It might not have had all the bells and whistles and the safety of the bank, the pension and some of that stuff, but I think it was a meaningful basic amount. And if you've had a year where you've been short-changed for your efforts…'

I asked Callum about his dealings with the police after Alistair's murder. He responded: 'The senior guy who was in touch with the bank was a guy called Jake Patience. I think they were all drug squad. That was their background, based in Inverness. I probably did more interviews with the police than anybody else at the bank. We went through files. The main guy I dealt with was from the west coast. He was pretty laid-back, a good guy. It would get a bit frustrating because he would chat away for forty minutes and then say, "Right, we better write some of this stuff up," and then you'd be repeating yourself as you went through every page. I didn't have any experience of what that thing [the investigation] should look like. I had nothing to benchmark it against, but my perception was these are not specialist murder investigation guys.'

My next question was an obvious one: 'What about their level of understanding of specialist financial matters, or their ability to grasp financial matters?'

Callum was clear: 'Layman's stuff, really. I say that with all due respect. We were kind of starting from scratch, to be honest with you. I certainly remember a couple of sessions looking at physical files. There were a few physical files that Alistair had had at home with him working that weekend, bearing in mind he was going to be leaving the bank in three weeks' time. I think at one point we retrieved all the physical files that myself and Alistair had worked on in that two-year period. We had them in an open office at the police headquarters and I was pretty much going through them with a couple of the guys. There would be a file on somebody buying a plot of land to build on, but they [the police] had no expertise on the dynamics of how a broker might come to a bank, or how a customer might, or what the credit process was when you declined them.'

I was a Scotland Yard drug squad officer once upon a time. We were pretty good at what we did, but I cannot think of a bunch of men and women who would have been less qualified to examine bank financial records, potentially looking for a murder motive, than us. Give us drugs, guns, international illicit dealings and we were fine. Complex financial matters, nah, we wouldn't have had a clue what we were looking at. The examination of these files should have been done by officers with some experience of the world of finance. Such officers did exist at the time, although possibly not in the Northern Constabulary. The City of London Police would have had copious amounts of detectives with specialisms in this field. They should have been drafted in.

'Would it be possible to hide or disguise something from the police investigation if somebody at the bank was so minded?' I probed.

Callum replied, 'Probably you could have. I remember there was a fella at the bank who dealt with invoice discounting. It's known as cash flow finances. Typically, this would be for businesses maybe involved in manufacturing or recruitment. These businesses might have a debtor book, so they've got customers who might pay in sixty days, seventy days, or fifty days, whatever it might be. It's a product where the bank would lend against an invoice note. With a good customer, the bank will advance that money, so they've got it in six days, but at a cost. Typically, where Alistair and myself had to get our deals done, this was almost a thirty-yarder because pound for pound, that brought in the bank a lot more profit instead of a boring old overdraft.'

Callum explained more about this facility: 'Although the

customer might need this for the first two or three months, their contract was with the bank for a year so it was remunerate for the bank. I'm not saying it was a bad product, but typically for me and Alistair to get our bonuses, we probably needed a couple of those deals over the course of a year. The point on this fella was he was an invoicing discount specialist and a really good guy, but he didn't get interviewed by the police for a couple of months. Alistair worked quite closely with him, particularly over the last year-and-a-half. He was probably the seventh or eighth in the bank who Alistair had the most contact with. I remember speaking to him at the time, thinking, how the hell have you not been interviewed? He just seemed to fall off the radar. There were bits of the [police] investigation that I thought about at the time. You'd scratch your head and think, really, where are they going with this?'

'Did their lack of understanding enable gaps in the investigation?'

Callum replied: 'They were well-meaning guys who didn't have the expertise. I think a lot of time we had to go right back to basics – how does a credit file get built? All the rest of it. A lot of time was spent on that. To me, it was a group of guys, more drug squad, petty crime, and they were caught out of their comfort zone. To me, it seemed a bit lacklustre. They were out of their depth when it came to what was required.'

My next question was perhaps an obvious one: 'Did they bring in any independent financial experts?'

'No,' was Callum's unequivocal reply.

I asked, 'If somebody was so minded in the Inverness operation, if Alistair was so minded, would it have been possible to conceal, to be dishonest, to act without integrity?'

Callum replied, 'I think you could, I think it was doable. It was certainly doable if you look what banking was like when I left in 2013. In our role as hunters, it was more difficult because you still had to hand over to a farmer. I think it's more likely if you had a hunter and a farmer colluding together...'

'How many farmers did Alistair pass files on to?' I enquired.

Callum responded, 'Maybe fourteen or fifteen across the north of Scotland. We would see them quite regularly.'

I asked if he thought Alistair might have had a corrupt relationship with any of them. Callum was clear in his reply: 'No, I don't see it at all.'

'Do you think Alistair's work had anything to do with his murder?' I asked.

'It's come into my mind.' There was then a lengthy pause, with a deep intake of breath by Callum, 'I suppose Alistair did, he was very work focused. So was I... I don't think he had a whole lot of spare time apart from work. So, unless we're going with the theory of some guy just happened to be on his doorstep, looking for an Alan Wilson two doors down, because work was such a large part of what he did, unless it was some complete secret life that I knew nothing of, another woman or whatever it may be, then I suppose in my mind since 28 November 2004, unless it was a completely random mistaken identity, then probably, in my mind, it's always been there, it's through work.'

'Can you think of anything in particular that it may have been?' I asked.

Callum replied, 'Never really could then, to be honest with you, or now. We went through every file, every diary, 2002,

2003, 2004… names in the margin. I couldn't really come up with anything compelling.'

I asked if Alistair had ever discussed his work in the specialist lending department, when he was based in Edinburgh. Callum couldn't recall him ever speaking about that time, nor had Alistair ever mentioned being involved in the lending of money to any football clubs.

'Could Alistair have gone to meetings with businesses, with business people alone, without another bank employee present?' I wanted to know.

Callum's response was swift: 'Yeah, without doubt. That was really part of the hunter gig.'

I asked if he was aware of Alistair taking out a loan or being lent a significant amount of money, either by the bank or anyone else: 'No. He had a mortgage on the big house, which they ran as a bed-and-breakfast/restaurant for some time. I was certainly aware of that. There were certain things with the house that didn't go to plan. They had to pay VAT on it to purchase it, which I think was quite an expense at the eleventh hour. There were certainly some issues with the house itself, there were some challenging windows on it. Veronica and the kids had to decamp to a caravan for about a month. There was some financial pressure. He certainly had a bigger mortgage than he wanted to have and budgeted on having…

'I remember speaking to one of the bosses, who said that Al hadn't claimed two or three months of expenses, probably from being too busy. But if every pound's a prisoner, you've probably got your expenses in on the first of every month, getting that cash back.'

Callum told me that the bosses were fairly generous when it came to expenses as they understood a good night out with a client was often money well spent. I found it rather puzzling that Alistair wasn't claiming those expenses back promptly. If money was tight, and it appeared it may have been, then why not get the cash back as soon as possible? Perhaps he had been in receipt of cash from elsewhere, thereby negating the need to worry about those expenses, which Callum told me could amount to around £120 per month? If so, it begs the question, where was that other money coming from? There have been media reports and rumours that Alistair borrowed some £50,000 from unscrupulous lenders, which I have not been able to confirm or otherwise dismiss. Could that have been money he was dipping into? Callum told me that because Alistair was not reclaiming expenses at the first possible opportunity, one of his bosses thought all must be well on the financial front.

Any such unofficial borrowing or other substantial payments to Alistair should have been fairly easy for the police to identify after his murder. A full and thorough examination of his spending patterns would have readily identified any changing trends. For example, if Alistair suddenly stopped making cash withdrawals that would indicate he had access to other funds. Similarly, with bills and shopping and other such expenditure. If Alistair began to pay these with cash, rather than by cheque, standing order or direct debit, that would be a clear indication he was sourcing ready cash from elsewhere and I would like to think that information would have been made public by the police. They couldn't honestly claim to have not discovered a motive if they'd come across that kind of information. We know Alistair had money in the bank and contributed to a savings scheme. Maybe all was well on the finances front and the reason for his murder defies all conventional logic.

Callum recalled a conversation he had with this colleague, when the topic of Alistair came up. He told me, 'He asked me how long I had worked with Alistair in a close role. I told him two-and-a-half years. He said, "You must have the patience of a fucking saint!" This other employee had found Alistair hard going, a bit aloof. It was totally missed by the police up here, getting to him early on.'

I've tried to contact Callum's colleague. I left answerphone messages and emailed him. He has not returned any of my communications.

My conversation with Callum was drawing towards a close. I asked him about the mutual back-scratching among bankers, lawyers and surveyors that I'd heard about. He replied, 'Yes, it happened in some cases. I wasn't charged for the valuation on my house up here. I don't think thousands of pounds would have been written off, but certainly, myself and Al had some discretion in terms of what fees could be charged to a client coming in. You could write off, you could say, "We'll only charge them half, because they can give me this other business over here." You would have certain dispensation.'

Building on what my source Angus had told me some months ago, I asked, 'Could you refund charges without anybody knowing?'

Callum replied, 'That would be true up to a certain level.'

Throughout this interview Callum had been forthright

and matter-of-fact. He hadn't displayed a lot of emotion. I thanked him for his time and his insight into Alistair and life at the bank. I knew I'd just been given more information than had ever reached the public domain. Callum told me he was keen to see justice because the murder of his former colleague still 'perplexes and niggles'.

I know how you feel, Callum!

CHAPTER TWENTY-SEVEN

NO PEACE FOR THE WICKED

Tom and I went for a bite to eat. We'd not long had breakfast, but he has a gargantuan appetite. He's a lot younger than me and cycles regularly so he stays in good shape.

After our early lunch we took a walk to the grassy links overlooking the beach and the Moray Firth. The sun was shining and it was an idyllic setting. It was the school holidays so many parents, grandparents and others were walking along the beach, playing and laughing with a huge number of children. Tom and I were sat on a bench within sight of Alistair Wilson's house. We talked about murder and television. I knew this was to be my last trip to Nairn for a while and I guess I was in a bit of a reflective mood.

A wave of emotion crept up on me that I could not suppress. I let it flow. First, I was angry, really angry, at the stealing of such a young life: only thirty years old, with a wife and two young boys. And then I became sad for Alistair, a man denied all the joy and unforgettable happiness that family life can bring. The kisses goodnight, the 'I love you' moments, the football, rugby, cricket, golf, holidays, helping with homework, mickey taking, life skills imparting, meeting of partners, grandchildren and more. Never to be for a man who did not deserve to die. When I told Tom how I was feeling, he was taken aback – I suspect he thought a seasoned former detective and crime writer would be immune to such feelings. I sat in silence for a while.

I had places to go and people to see. Hoteliers, café owners, sources and more, all of them had to be thanked. During this mini tour, a member of the public posed the question, 'Have you solved it?' I've been asked this question many times and of course I have to admit that I haven't, not yet anyway. To have indisputably named Alistair Wilson's killer within these pages would have been astonishing. Maybe it will happen one day. My objectives to keep this case in the public domain, to send out a clear message to the killer and put new information into the public domain have all been achieved. Now, I wait. I wait to see if more people will come forward, if the police decide they do finally want to talk to me and whether Veronica Wilson wants to sit down with me.

Please accept my apology if this book has raised more questions than it answered. Such is the risk I take when embarking on a project like this. I appreciate there are still aspects of this crime that do not appear to make sense. Maybe, just maybe, as minds far greater than mine have said, maybe it doesn't all have to make sense. If, however, you feel like you've been short-changed then I do apologise. This project was always going to be more the beginning of a quest than the end. And as I've always said on social media, on the radio or in the papers, if there's anything you want to say, let's talk.

Here, I feel compelled to write a few words for any remaining sceptics who may still be out there. Flawed as the Northern Constabulary's investigation was, I think it is overwhelmingly likely that in a town as small as Nairn, any secret lover, hidden fortune, payment to a gunman or otherwise concealed motive or tiny shred of evidence linking Veronica Wilson to the murder of her husband would invariably have been found – and it hasn't been.

Many of you have commented on Veronica's decision to remain at 10 Crescent Road after the killing – well, that was her choice to make, not ours. And while many more have observed how strange you thought that decision was, I will reiterate, strange does not in any way equate to guilt.

I agree with some people who have pored over Veronica's statements of 2017 and think it is very odd that she used the word 'gentleman' to describe the gunman. If somebody shot my wife dead, I very much doubt I would describe them in that way! Maybe she fears that he could come back so she chose not to use any inflammatory language, we just don't know. Let's face it, the police have not done her and the boys the best favour of all and caught the gunman, have they? The truth is we just cannot put ourselves in Veronica's shoes. We have not had to experience what she has gone through, not only on that night but for the past fourteen years. Cut the woman some well-deserved slack.

On the last night of my trip, I finally got to watch Nairn County Football Club. They were playing away against Keith

FC, about a forty-minute drive away. Tom and I made the journey down there on a bitterly cold April night to watch a thoroughly entertaining 2–2 draw. I've even got myself a Nairn scarf and now I will always look out for their results. We returned to our hotel to see Veronica and a friend sitting at the bar, enjoying a drink and a chat. Naturally, and rightly so, we did not make an approach. Maybe one day we will speak, but in the meantime, I wish her and her boys all the very best.

And finally, at least for the time being, a message to a murderer…

I anguished long and hard about how I should start this letter to you. 'Dear Killer' didn't seem right, nor did 'Hi Gunman' or 'Hello Murderer'. Actually, it isn't really anguish at all, is it? No, anguish is what you've caused Veronica Wilson and the boys for the past fourteen years. But I wanted to get this message right, because I'm utterly convinced that one way or another, you'll get to read this.

This book has received quite a bit of publicity, so unless you're living a laid-back life on some remote beach in the middle of nowhere, (which I don't think you are), I'm sure you'll have heard about it. And you won't have been able to resist the temptation to look inside these pages: you'll want to know what I know.

I doubt whether you've paid for this book – you don't strike me as that kind of person. I suspect you've probably shoplifted it or stolen it from a library. Maybe you've borrowed this book from a friend or a relative; less likely perhaps because I doubt you live a life full of love and affection, of shared Sunday lunches and Christmas dinners where wine flows, along with engaging conversations and bellicose laughs, creating memories to last a lifetime. I doubt you have that kind of life.

I doubt you enjoy children on your lap. I doubt you enjoy the indestructible memories of putting the kids to bed, of caring for them when they're poorly, or the love they lavish upon you so often just because they can. Do you care that you won't be grieved for, missed and or spoken about once you're gone? Probably not, because you're not like me and the people I spend my life with.

A major reason you don't enjoy the things that I and many millions more do is because of your actions on the evening of 28 November 2004. Try as hard as you do to move on and find some kind of utterly fulfilling life for yourself, you just can't. That night remains a dark secret, which became an itch and over the years has festered into a raging open sore that will not heal, no matter how much you try to move on. Sure, you can keep your actions hidden and you've done that remarkably well, but there's a price to pay for that, which is lasting, fulfilling happiness denied. You have only yourself to blame. Go on, admit it, your actions that night have prevented you from moving on, haven't they? You might even feel that because you haven't truly progressed in life, that you've been punished enough, but you haven't. Not in the eyes of Veronica, the boys and the nation at large.

Credit where it's due, you've done a remarkable job of evading capture for a very long time, although the police investigation wasn't exactly the best, was it? I'm sure you probably think that as shallow as your existence is, your life has been better for not being in jail. So be it. But you must be just a bit concerned by this book and the renewed police activity. Even if you're sitting somewhere laughing your socks off at me because I am so far away from the actual truth, remember this: thousands of people are going to read this book. Many people will contact me with theories, thoughts, gossip and rumour. And maybe, just maybe, amongst all of that will be the incontrovertible truth.

This case is not going away, and nor am I. As I said at the start of this book I will not give up. Please do not take that as a threat, for I'm not in the business of threatening anybody, but it is a promise.

I do really hope we meet one day, and I'm sure we will. If and when that hole in your soul, that gaping, festering wound becomes a burden too heavy to bear, then call me, or the cops. Can I hear you laughing at me once again?

Please remember, we are on this planet for such a short time that we should strive to do some good while we're here. If the killing of Alistair Wilson is the stand out moment of your life, they can't exactly put that on your headstone, can they? So, how about you put the record straight? You might then earn a reputation amongst some, certainly me, for being someone who finally did the right thing. At the moment that decision is yours to make. Things may change. That opportunity may one day be denied to you.

Till we meet,
Peter Bleksley
Facebook – Peter Bleksley
Twitter – @peterbleksley